b2514891n

SAN MATEO CITY PUBLIC LIBRARY
3 9047 02727749 6
D0535118

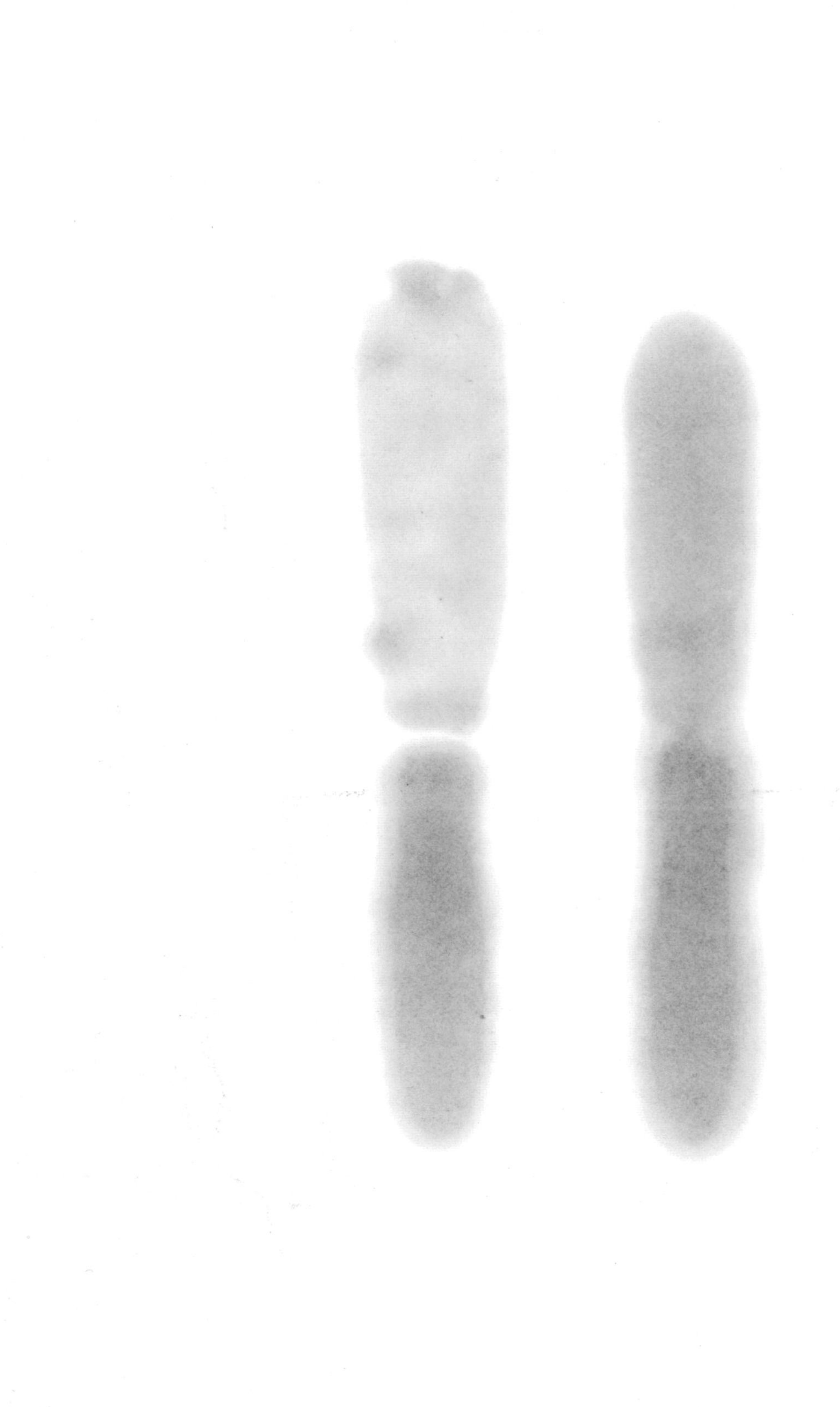

REDWOODS
The World's Largest Trees

REDWOODS

The World's Largest Trees

Jeremy Joan Hewes

RAND McNALLY & COMPANY

A Bison Book

REDWOODS

Published in the United States by Rand McNally & Company, 1981

First published in the UK by Bison Books Limited

Produced by
Bison Books Limited
4 Cromwell Place
London SW7

Printed in Hong Kong

ISBN: 0-528-81543-1
Library of Congress Catalog
Card Number: 81-50175

Project director: Bill Henkin
Book design: Jon Goodchild
Editor: Suzanne Lipsett

Excerpt from *The Last Redwoods and the Parklands of Redwood Creek,* by Francois Leydet. Copyright ©1969 by the Sierra Club. Reprinted by permission of the Sierra Club.

Photographs on page 38 reprinted with the permission of the publisher from *The White Redwoods—Ghosts of the Forest* by Douglas F Davis and Dale F Holderman. Copyright ©1979 by Naturegraph Publishers Inc, California.

Illustrations on pages 37, 48, 49, 75, 79 & 165 reproduced courtesy of Save-the-Redwoods-League. Photograph on p 37 by Howard King, copyright ©1978 by Save-the-Redwoods-League. Photographs and diagrams of pps 48 & 49 from *Story Told by a Fallen Redwood* by Emanuel Fritz, copyright ©1978 by Save-the-Redwoods-League. Photographs on pps 75, 76 & 79 from *Redwoods of the Past* by Ralph W Chaney, reproduced by permission of Save-the-Redwoods-League.

Photograph on page 156 (right) from *Grand and Ancient Forest* by Carolyn de Vries. Reprinted by permission of the author.

Illustration on page 124 reprinted with the permission of the publisher from *An Everyday History of Somewhere* by Ray Rafael. Illustration by Mark Livingston, copyright ©1974 by Ray Rafael. Reprinted by permission of Island Press, California.

THE WORLD'S LARGEST TREES

'It has been said that trees are imperfect men, and seem to bemoan their imprisonment rooted in the ground. But they never seem so to me. I never saw a discontented tree. They grip the ground as though they liked it, and though fast rooted they travel about as far as we do. They go wandering forth in all directions with every wind, going and coming like ourselves, traveling with us around the sun two million miles a day, and through space heaven knows how fast and far!'

—John Muir

CONTENTS

INTRODUCTION

Below: The coast redwood (*Sequoia sempervirens*); the giant sequoia (*Sequoiadendron giganteum*), also called the Big Tree or Sierra redwood; and the dawn redwood (*Metasequoia glyptostroboides*), sometimes called the water larch.

Redwood trees count among them the world's largest and the world's tallest living things. These colossal dimensions are not exhibited by all redwood trees, however; nor are they restricted to one type of redwood. Rather, two distinct trees are commonly called redwoods. The two types live several hundred miles apart, and—except for similarities in color of bark and heartwood—they do not even look like close relatives.

Perhaps the tree most widely known by the name redwood is *Sequoia sempervirens,* the coast redwood, which supplies the great majority of redwood lumber and was the first sequoia discovered. This species claims the tallest known standing tree. Called simply Tall Tree, this sentinel measures 367.8 feet in height and a slender 10 feet in diameter 5 feet above the ground. Discovered in 1963 by members of the National Geographic Society, the Tall Tree grows in a grove near the Pacific Coast in northern California, in what is now Redwood National Park. If cut, this tree would yield 121,480 board feet (a board foot is 1 foot long, 1 foot wide, 1 inch thick) of timber, enough for eight five-room homes. Tall Tree was accurately measured in 1968; before that time a 359-foot specimen in Rockefeller Forest on Bull Creek Flat vied for the honor of world's tallest tree with the Founder's Tree on Dyerville Flat, which had been slated at 364 feet but was remeasured and found to be less than 359 feet tall. All of these trees are now protected in the parklands of California.

The most massive trees on earth, both in circumference and volume, are of the *Sequoiadendron giganteum.* These are the giant sequoias, often called the Big Tree or Sierra redwood, of the Sierra Nevada mountains of California. The largest specimen of this sequoia, known as the General Sherman Tree, measures 101.6 feet in circumference at its base and weighs an estimated 12 million pounds; its height is a comparatively modest 272.4 feet. If cut for lumber, this single tree would yield 600,120 board feet, the makings of 40 five-room houses. The giant sequoia is no longer used for timber, though, because its wood is too brittle for most commercial purposes.

Both of these magnificent trees are native to the western United States, and since the Ice Age their ranges have been strictly limited to narrow strips in California (and, for the coast redwood, a tiny corner of southwestern Oregon). Before the glacial sweep, a botanical cousin of these trees, the dawn redwood *(Metasequoia glyptostroboides),* flourished along with sequoias in many areas of the world, and in 1944 living specimens of this relatively small tree (maximum height, 140 feet) were found in a remote area of central China. All three types of redwoods have been cultivated successfully in other parts of the world, but the propagated varieties attain only a fraction of the size commanded by the California trees.

The unique stature and age of California's existing redwoods—up to 3500 years for giant sequoia, up to 2200 years old for coast redwoods—have won the respect of foresters, the praise of poets, and the fervent prayers of conservationists. More important, these trees have won protection. Virtually all remaining giant sequoias are held in public trust, and most virgin coast redwoods (ancient, uncut specimens) are similarly protected in parklands, although the ripple effects of logging on neighboring commercial properties still endanger some of the largest and oldest protected trees. Dedicated defenders of these irreplaceable forests continue their efforts to expand the boundaries of redwood preserves and to blunt the impact of logging on the trees' fragile environment. Protection from human interference has been extended for barely a century and thus seems a modest gesture toward an awesome natural treasure that has stood for more than 3000 years.

TREE LIFE

Earth's forests contain thousands of species of trees, each of which is distinguished by the individual characteristics of its seeds, leaves and growth. Regardless of species, however, all trees have the same general structure and requirements for survival. They all utilize water, soil, air and light to manufacture food, increase in size and produce seeds.

The root system of a tree, which in redwoods is 4 to 6 feet deep and as much as 250 feet wide, collects water and minerals from the soil. Root tips are protected with a hard covering that enables them to probe the soil both vertically and laterally. Microscopic root hairs cover the root's surface and literally embrace grains of earth from which they absorb moisture and nutrients.

The root system sends the water and dissolved minerals to the leaves of the tree, where food production takes place. The leaves, in turn, send food back down to the roots, which cannot produce any nutrients on their own. All this transporting of substances takes place through the trunk and branches, where the wood is arranged in several layers that have specific functions in the process.

The outermost layer of the tree, the bark, provides protection for the plant; this layer is made up of dead and aging cells that formerly served as conduits for food. The inner bark is the active food transport system, called the phloem, and this layer also stores food for the tree. Beneath the phloem is the cambium, the only part of the trunk that produces new cells. The cambium layer is microscopically thin, its cells continually dividing to add new growth to the layers on either side of it. The cambium does not add to the height of

Opposite: The human form is dwarfed by the huge boles and hollow bases of giant sequoia trees.

Left: A swamp cypress tree, of the family Taxodiaceae, to which redwood trees also belong. When redwoods were first discovered, some botanists wanted to assign them to the swamp cypress genus (*Taxodium*), rather than creating a new genus for these trees.

THE ANATOMY & GROWTH OF TREES

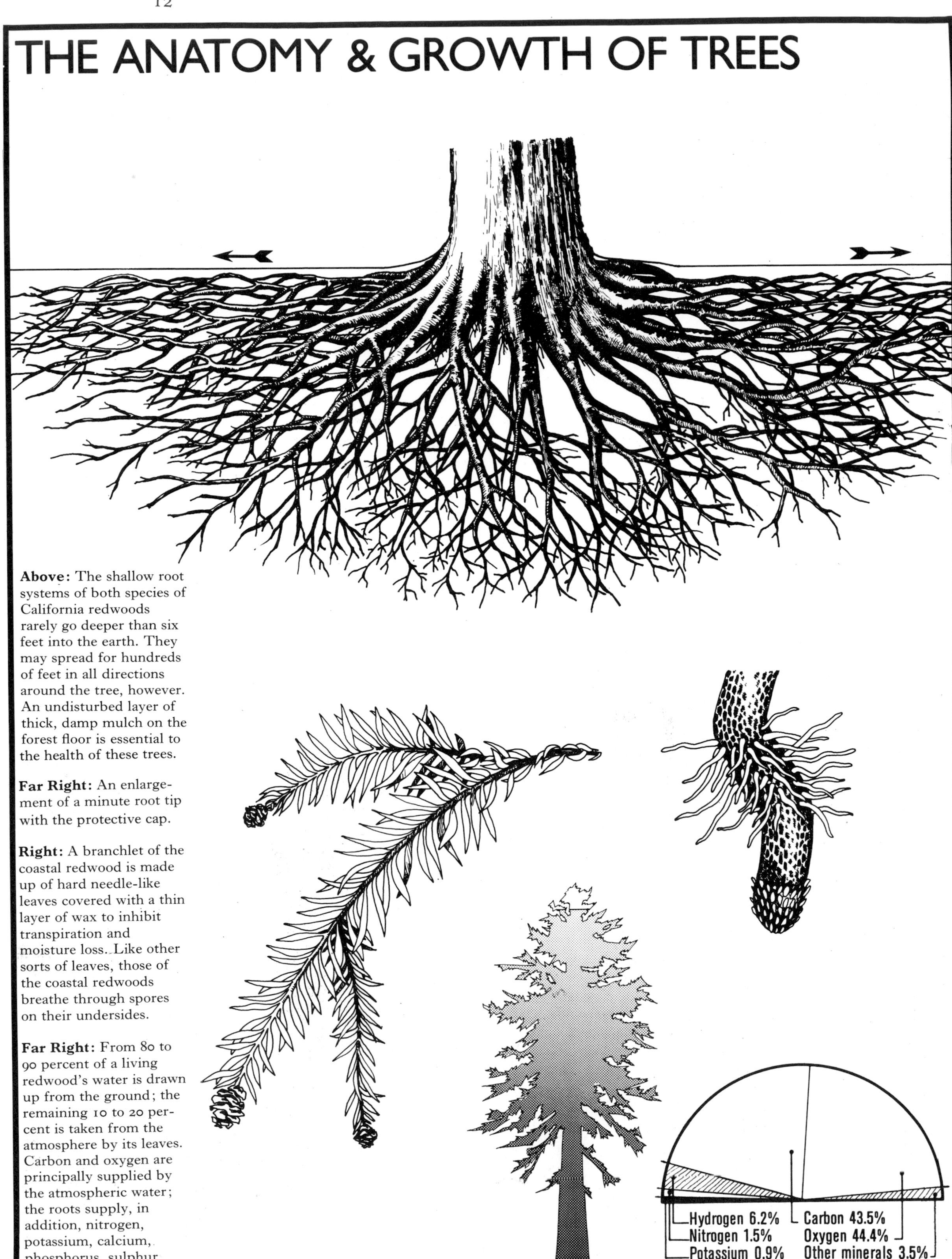

Above: The shallow root systems of both species of California redwoods rarely go deeper than six feet into the earth. They may spread for hundreds of feet in all directions around the tree, however. An undisturbed layer of thick, damp mulch on the forest floor is essential to the health of these trees.

Far Right: An enlargement of a minute root tip with the protective cap.

Right: A branchlet of the coastal redwood is made up of hard needle-like leaves covered with a thin layer of wax to inhibit transpiration and moisture loss. Like other sorts of leaves, those of the coastal redwoods breathe through spores on their undersides.

Far Right: From 80 to 90 percent of a living redwood's water is drawn up from the ground; the remaining 10 to 20 percent is taken from the atmosphere by its leaves. Carbon and oxygen are principally supplied by the atmospheric water; the roots supply, in addition, nitrogen, potassium, calcium, phosphorus, sulphur, iron and magnesium.

the tree, but adds to its diameter; all upward growth is accomplished by the tips of the branches.

The xylem, or sapwood, of a tree carries water from the roots to the leaves. Like the phloem, this layer also stores food as a reserve supply for the tree, and it receives new cells from the neighboring cambium. As the xylem ages, its water-movement function ceases, and this woody layer becomes heartwood, which constitutes the real strength of the tree. The heartwood is no longer living, but it will stay intact so long as the layers of cells around it continue to be nourished.

It is the heartwood and sapwood layers that reveal a tree's record of growth. The rings that are visible in any cut log or stump show the annual growth of that tree; their dark outside edges represent the summer growth of small cells, and the wider, lighter-colored interior section of each ring record the spring growth, which is less dense and made up of larger cells than those produced in summer. In very old trees, particularly the giant sequoia, the number of growth rings can be misleading. In some instances an annual ring may not have reached the level of the stump, because the rings begin at the tree's crown. In other instances, the pattern of growth rings may be distorted owing to a fire scar or a buttress on one side of the trunk.

Water and dissolved minerals flow through the roots and trunk of the tree in a continuous process known as transpiration. For the most part, the leaves (or needles, which are a conifer's leaves) pull the water upward through the tree's body as they release water from their many pores through evaporation. This process of upward movement is aided by the surface tension of water molecules in the tree's circulatory system. Water moving upward through the sapwood could be likened to the column of mercury in a thermometer; its molecules cling together as they move up or down in the narrow chamber inside the instrument. The water in the long vertical cells of the sapwood behaves similarly, forming an unbroken column from roots to leaves.

At its destination, the water meets chlorophyll, stored in the leaves in millions of cell bodies called chloroplasts. When carbon dioxide from the air and sunlight also reach the chlorophyll, photosynthesis occurs. In this chemical reaction, the life-giving process for the tree, carbon dioxide and water combine to form

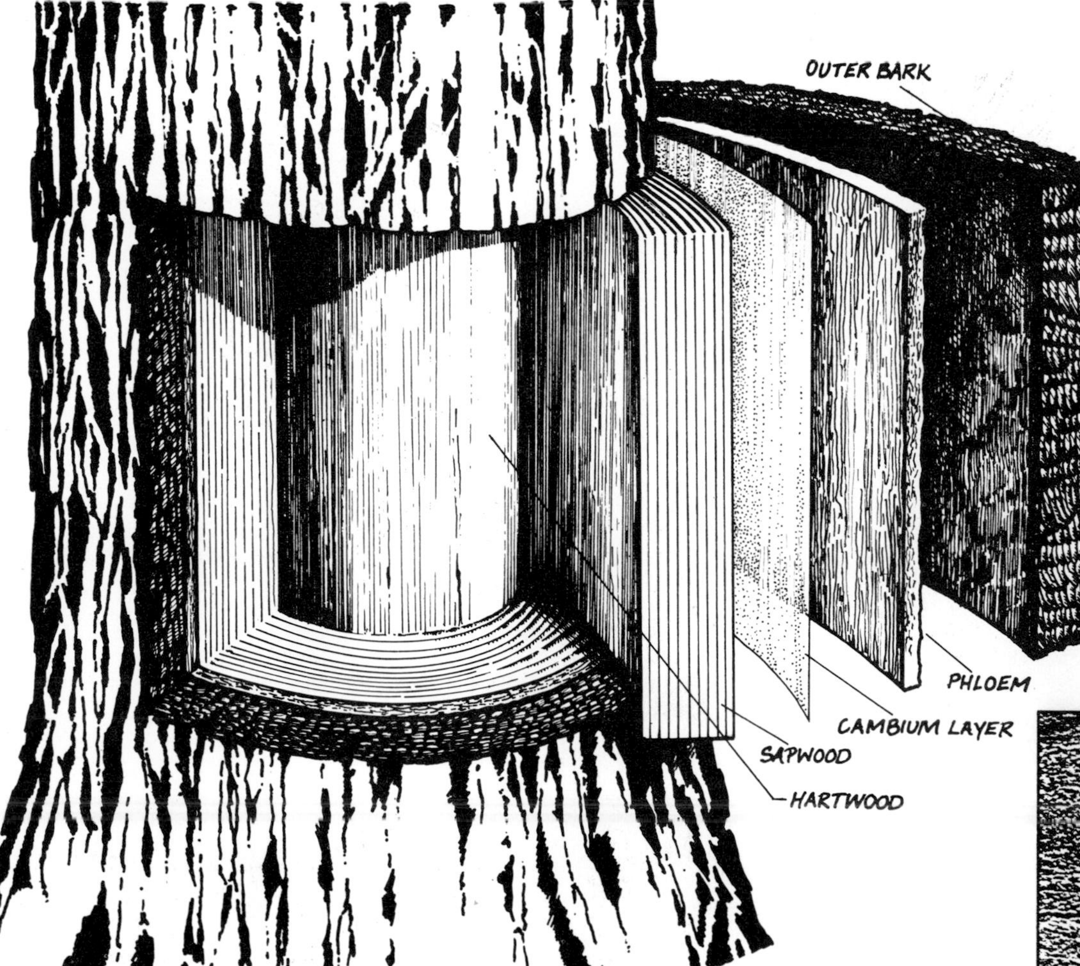

Left: Even a hollow redwood tree may continue to live for centuries, as long as the living tissue outside its core fulfills the tree's vital needs. The tubes and fibers within the heartwood are inert, and serve the tree only as reinforcement.

Below: The typical cellular structure of the coastal redwood. The lightweight, straight-grained, non-resinous timber has conspicuous growth rings; it is a moderately strong commercial softwood.

glucose, the food for the tree. Oxygen, a by-product of photosynthesis, is released into the atmosphere to sustain all nonplant forms of life. The chemical formula for this process is as follows:

$$6CO_2 + 6H_2O + \text{energy} \rightarrow C_6H_{12}O_6 + 6O_2$$

carbon dioxide — water — sunlight — glucose — oxygen

In addition to the products of photosynthesis, each leaf gives off excess water through its underside, adding moisture to the air and keeping the temperature of the leaf cool enough for photosynthesis to continue. Thus, through the combined actions of transpiration and photosynthesis, trees actually increase the moisture in an area, by raising the water table through the action of their roots and by recycling water into the air through their leaves.

Below: The coast redwood thrives in a moist sea of greenery, which surrounds the man standing among these widely spaced trees.

CONIFERS: THE WORLD'S TIMBER

REDWOODS ARE CONIFERS, a category of trees and shrubs so named because they produce cones that carry the tree's seeds. Most conifers are also called evergreens, for the reason that they retain their needle-shaped leaves year-round. (Trees that lose their leaves annually are called deciduous, although neither classification is without exception; for example, the dawn redwood, though a conifer, is deciduous.) Conifers do replace their leaves, however; this is done in a rotating fashion, with all the leaves being replaced at least every few years.

Among the other general characteristics of conifers are their soft wood and long, straight trunks, which make them ideal sources of timber. These trees supply three-fourths of the world's lumber and almost all the pulp for its paper. (Hardwood trees, such as oak, maple, cherry and walnut, supply the remaining one-fourth of the world's lumber, much of which is used for furniture and decorative trim and veneers.) Other important timber trees among the conifers are the Douglas fir, perhaps the most utilized and valuable source of commercial wood because of its strength and large size; the longleaf pine, used in paper products and construction materials; and the ponderosa pine, used in both rough construction and fine finishing such as panelling and trim. Altogether some 450 species of conifers survive, many of them cultivated as commercial timber crops.

Conifers are limited to the northern sector of the temperate zone of the planet, an area covering the northern United States, Canada, much of Europe and northern Asia. Their territory has diminished greatly since the beginnings of sophisticated plant life, for conifers were the first trees to develop and formed the dominant type of forest 100 million years ago. The epoch in which they thrived—called the Age of Conifers, in the Jurassic period of geologic history—spanned some 30 million years. Gradually the early hardwood (deciduous) trees developed, such as beeches, maples and dogwoods, and the forests became mixed in most places.

'In most places' is indeed accurate, since forests virtually covered the globe until about a million years ago. At that time the earth began to cool radically, and the Ice Age took over, sending trees into retreat across the continents. As the glaciers moved southward, they decimated many types of conifers and deciduous trees; Europe lost nearly all of its native species in this period. North America was affected less drastically, and the native sequoia species managed to survive, although the altered climate after the Ice Age limited their range to two small strips of earth.

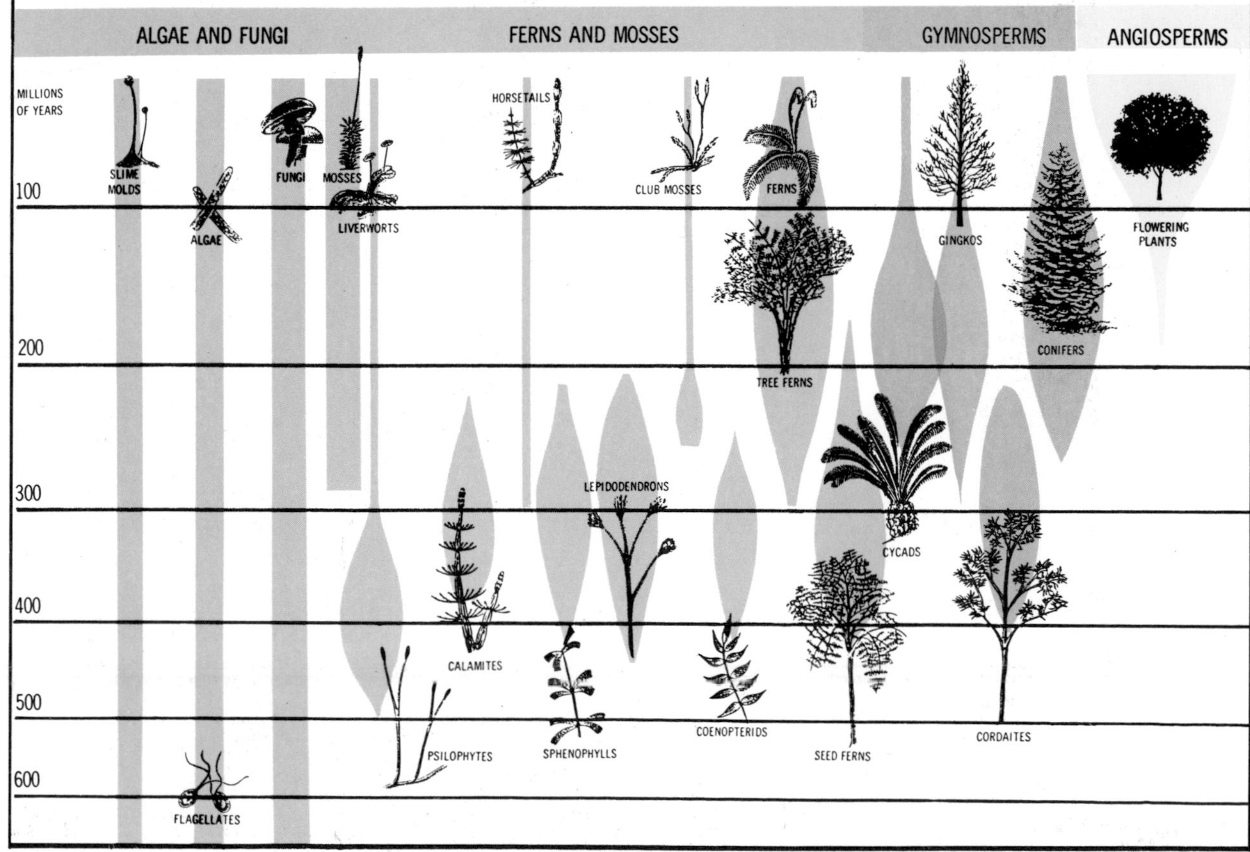

Left: Plants evolved on earth from the unicellular ancestors of all life through several botanically simple forms to the Age of Conifers, some 200 million years ago. Redwoods and all conifers are gymnosperms, plants that release their seeds without any protective coating or shell. Most deciduous trees, which developed after conifers, are angiosperms, plants that produce their seeds in fruit or some other protective device and only release them as part of this whole package.

THE REDWOOD FAMILY

Coniferales, to which conifers belong, is an order within the classification system of plants. It is a subcategory of two larger groupings, the division Spermatophyta, or seed-bearing plants, and the class Coniferospida. The order Coniferales is further subdivided into families, genera and species.

The redwood trees are members of the family Taxodiaceae, which is often called the deciduous cypress family, probably because one of its distinctive members, the bald or swamp cypress, sheds its leaves yearly. The trees in this family are characterized by round cones and narrow, needlelike leaves. Other family members include the dawn redwood, the Japanese umbrella pine, the Japanese cedar, the Chinese fir and the Tasmanian cedar.

In addition to the three species of redwood that are well established, a few cultivated varieties are now being planted as ornamental trees in many parts of the world. These include the weeping sequoia, a varietal of *Sequoiadendron giganteum* whose odd shapes and clinging foliage have inspired the name 'the ugliest tree in Britain.' Another sequoia form, the *aureum,* is also cultivated in England and is distinguished by variegated yellow leaves.

Certain trees are mistaken for redwoods because of their color and appearance. Two species commonly called redwoods but not botanically related to sequoias are the Amazonia, a Brazilian tree with light red and orange wood, and the Andaman redwood, from Burma and the Andaman Islands, which has red or crimson wood streaked with red. The wood from another tree unrelated to sequoias, the Scots pine *(Pinus sylvestris),* is often referred to as redwood lumber in Europe.

Opposite: 'Cousins' of the redwoods, these other members of the Taxodiaceae family are the Chinese swamp cypress; Japanese umbrella pine; Chinese fir; Japanese cedar; and Tasmanian cedar.

DIVISION	ORDER	FAMILY
GYMNOSPERMS	CYCADELE	Tree ferns
	GINKGOALE	Ginkgo
	TAXALE	Yew, Plum yew
	CONIFERALE	Yellow wood, Chile pine, Cypress, SWAMP CYPRESS, Pine/Fir/Spruce
ANGIOSPERMS	DI-COTYLEDON	Magnolia, Laurel, Beech/Oak, Elm, Birch, Hazel, Tea, Willow, Heather, Rose, Pea, Myrtle, Holly, Buckeye, Maple, Cashew, Citrus, Olive, Mahogany, etc.
	MONO-COTYLEDON	Lily, Palm

TAXODIACEAE

GENUS	SPECIES
TAXODIUM	Swamp bald cypress Pond cypress Montezuma bald cypress
GLYPTOSTROBUS	Chinese swamp cypress Weeping cypress
METASEQUOIA	Dawn redwood
SEQUOIA	Coastal redwood
SEQUOIADENDRON	Giant redwood
SCIADOPITYS	Japanese umbrella pine
CUNNINGHAMIA	Chinese 'fir'
CRYTOMERIA	Japanese cedar
TIAWANIA	Tiawan crytomeria
ATHROTAXUS	King William pine Tasmanian cedar Tasmanian cypress

Right: The basic tree families, with the Taxodiaceae family subdivided into its genera and species. As their common names indicate, many of these trees are native to Asia.

Below: The Scots pine (*Pinus sylvestris*) is found in Europe and Asia, as well as Britain; it is often mistakenly called a form of redwood because of its wood's color.

NAMING: THE BATTLE OF THE BOTANISTS

Before the sequoias were classified precisely, they were named for their most obvious feature—color. Both the bark and the wood of these trees, and especially the coast redwood, are reddish-brown in color. The first report of these coastal trees by European explorers was found in the journal of Franciscan missionary Fray Juan Crespi, who, in 1769, accompanied the expedition led by the Spanish explorer Portola north from Baja California to the Monterey area. Crespi described 'very high trees of a red color, not known to us' near Monterey on 10 October 1769 and drew the logical—and lasting—conclusion that 'because none of the expedition recognizes them, they are named redwood from their color.' Another Spanish missionary, serving as diarist for the expedition led by the explorer Anza in 1776, noted a single tall redwood 'rising like a great tower' alongside a creek south of San Francisco Bay. This tree was called *palo alto*—tall tree—and is located in the city that now bears its name.

Deriving the scientific names for the redwoods proved a far more complex problem than assigning descriptive terms or naming towns after trees. The first botanical examination of redwoods was begun in 1794, when Scottish botanist Archibald Menzies collected samples of the foliage, cones and seeds during an expedition along the coast of California. Menzies took the coast redwood samples to the herbarium of the Natural History Museum of London for study, but no scientific name was proposed for the new tree until 1828, when English botanist A B Lambert placed it in the genus *Taxodium*, the same as the bald cypress. He added the species name *sempervirens*, 'everliving,' because of the tree's year-round foliage and its ability to generate sprouts from its base.

Another botanist, Austrian Stephen Endlicher, disagreed with Lambert's designation of the coast redwood as a member of the *Taxodium* group. Instead, Endlicher proposed a new generic name for this tree, *Sequoia*. Although the Austrian botanist's own diaries do not confirm this speculation (and apparently no one asked him at the time, or at least made a record of such a conversation), Endlicher is believed to have chosen the name *Sequoia* because of his admiration for an American Indian, the Chero-

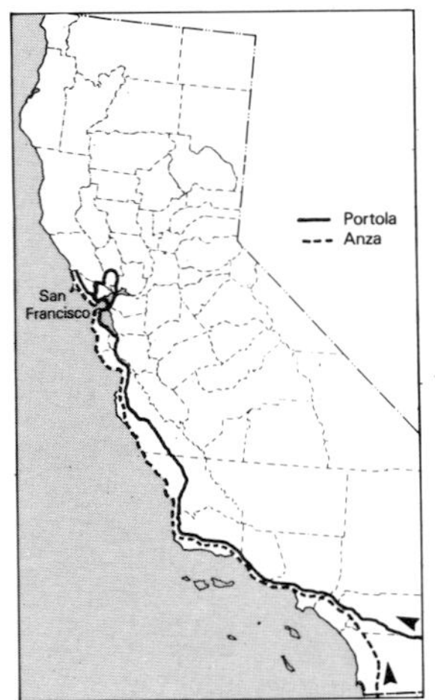

Above: Routes of the expeditions of Portola and Anza following earlier explorations by Drake (1579) and Vizciano (1602). Anza led the first colonists to San Francisco Bay in 1776.

Above: Archibald Menzies (1754–1842), the first botanist to see the colossal forests of virgin coast redwoods.

Right: A good example of young trees sprouting from the base of coast redwoods.

kee half-breed Sequoyah.

Whether or not Endlicher was really honoring Sequoyah, the Cherokee leader was worthy of such a tribute. He was born in Tennessee in 1760, the son of a Cherokee mother and a German immigrant father who left the family when the boy was quite young. This fatherless status and a crippling accident left him an outcast as a child, and Sequoyah determined to improve his own situation and that of his people. His major contribution was creating a written language for the Cherokee, and tirelessly helping other tribes to read and write in their own language. Sequoyah died alone in the Mexican Sierra, with no ceremony or marker to signal his passing.

Left: A T Dowd shooting a bear. Dowd discovered the two Calaveras groves of giant sequoia after wounding a grizzly bear and tracking it through the surrounding forest.

Far left: Sequoyah, after whom the trees are thought to be named. He was a halfbreed Cherokee who invented an 85-character alphabet for his tribe (shown below).

ᎡᎠᎳᏥᏀᏭᏯᏂᏁ
ᎸᎩᎼᏏᎵᏋᎹᎴᏬᏫ
ᏔᏴᏆᎯᏅᏲᎱᎪᏠ
ᏧᎽᏎᏖᏟᏩᏇᏌᏆᏃ
ᏌᏨᏒᏂᏚᏙᎰᎬ
ᎧᎢᎤᏰᏝᏣᎫᏦᏉᏱ
ᎾᏮᎶᏖᏮᎦᏕᏟ
ᎥᏅᏏᏧᏋᏆᏢᎰᎻᏝ
ᏊᏳᏗᏞᎿᏇᏜᎺᏋ

The state of Oklahoma did belatedly claim Sequoyah as an outstanding citizen, however, and his statue is one of two representing the state in the Statuary Hall in Washington, DC.

Endlicher proposed the name *Sequoia* about fifteen years after the death of Sequoyah, and most researchers have accepted the unconfirmed connection between the terms as true, or at least fitting. Yet the Austrian botanist's pronouncement of this conifer's genus was just the first volley in a battle of nomenclature that outlived both the namesake Sequoyah and the namegiver, Endlicher, who died in 1849. The real storm began when the Sierra trees were reported in 1852; one source labels the ensuing argument a 'remarkable illustration of departure from the accepted rules of botanical nomenclature.'

In 1852, the man who discovered one of the two Calaveras groves of giant sequoia in Calaveras County, A T Dowd, sent specimens of the tree to Albert Kellogg, a founder of San Francisco's Academy of Sciences. Kellogg and a colleague at the academy, D H Behr, studied the material but did not suggest a scientific name until three years later, in 1855. For unknown reasons, their conclusion bypassed Endlicher's designation of the genus *Sequoia,* instead assigning the Sierra redwood to the genus *Taxodium,* or bald cypress, and adding the species name *giganteum.*

The reason for the two American botanists' delay in naming the tree is not known, but they were generous in showing their specimens to visiting scientists during the three-year interval. One English naturalist, William Lobb, saw Kellogg's samples in 1853 and immediately journeyed to the Calaveras grove himself. He collected a supply of cones, seeds and foliage and returned to the nursery for which he was gathering specimens for cultivation. Lobb showed the samples to the noted English botanist John Lindley, who promptly published a description of the tree and its first 'official' name in the *Gardener's Chronicle* of December 1853. Lindley named the giant trees *Wellingtonia gigantea,* to honor the Duke of Wellington, because, the botanist wrote, the California tree towers above the forest 'as Wellington towers above his contemporaries.'

This British naming of an American native tree that neither Lindley nor Wellington had seen enraged American botanists, who countered with the names *Taxodium washingtonianum* and *Washingtonia californica,* both suggested by C F Winslow. The American supporters of these designations pointed out that the American hero Washington at least liked trees, which Wellington reputedly did not.

French botanist Joseph Decaisne entered this confusion of chauvinistic nomenclature, asserting that the coast and Sierra redwoods belonged to the same genus and that Endlicher's term *Sequoia* was botanically more accurate than any nationalistic epithet. (There is some speculation, but no proof, that the Frenchman was also motivated by chauvinistic feelings in his dismissal of the name of the man who had defeated Napoleon at Waterloo.) Decaisne retained Lindley's species name *gigantea,* and gradually botanists in Europe and America accepted this designation. The recognition of two national heroes has thus been erased from the tree's scientific name, but the English have kept their association with the military leader, for cultivated forms of giant sequoia are commonly called wellingtonia in Britain even today.

Curiously, the American scientists did not succeed in naming their most famous trees during this botanical rivalry. Kellogg and Behr's belated suggestion was less precise than Endlicher's or Decaisne's, and the commemoration of George Washington simply didn't take hold. Subsequently, however, one American made an important revision in the naming of redwood trees; in 1938, botanist John Buchholz noted differences in the embryology of the coast and Sierra trees, and he pointed out some 50 other variations between the species. Thus, he proposed a new generic name for the Sierra tree, *Sequoiadendron giganteum,* which came to be officially accepted.

Comparison of the coast (**right**) and Sierra (**far right**) redwoods. The green dense growth of the coast trees is distinct from the more open stand of Sierra sequoias, and the grayish bark of the coast tree contrasts with the rich cinnamon color of the Sierra redwoods.

Right: Comparison of dawn redwood, coast redwood and giant sequoia. Adapted from Hartesveldt et al., *The Giant Sequoia of the Sierra Nevada.*

	Dawn Redwood *(Metasequoia glyptostroboides)*	**Coast Redwood** *(Sequoia sempervirens)*	**Giant Sequoia** *(Sequoiadendron giganteum)*
Size:	Height—to 140 ft	to about 370 ft	to about 310 ft
	Diameter—to 6 ft	to 35 ft	
Leaves:	Needle-like	two types; needle-like and awl-shaped	awl-shaped
	with small stalk	sessile	sessile
	deciduous	persistent	persistent
Long branchlets:	Bear short shoots in opposite pairs	bear short shoots in alternate array	bear short shoots in alternate array
Short branchlets	Leaves opposite	leaves in spirals	leaves in spirals
	leaves in two rows	leaves in two rows except at tips	
	deciduous	deciduous	deciduous
Seed Cones:	About 1 inch long deciduous	0.75-1.50 inches long	2-3 inches long
		some persistent but open after first season	persistent and may remain green 20 years
	scales opposite	scales in spirals	scales in spirals
	seeds in one row on each scale	seeds in one row on each scale	seeds in two rows on each scale
	mature in one season	mature in one season	mature in two seasons
Pollen Cones (staminate):	Scales opposite	scales spiral	scales spiral
Buds:	scaly	scaly	naked
Chromosomes:	22 per diploid cell	66 per diploid cell	22 per diploid cell

Opposite: Early summer among the coast redwoods. The fog-filled spaces between trees provide an ideal growing environment for this moisture-loving tree. The unique geology and topography of the redwoods' habitat often leaves them bathed in fog when sunshine prevails everywhere beyond their groves.

THE WORLD'S TALLEST AND LARGEST

Opposite: The Wawona Tree, in an 1887 painting. The tunnel was cut in this tree in 1881, enlarging an existing fire scar. Two men were paid $75 for the job. The tree had a slight lean before the tunnel was cut; the tunnel increased the lean, until the 2300-year-old tree fell in 1969 under a 2-ton load of snow on its crown.

WHATEVER THE DISPUTES AMONG SCIENTISTS about the correct names for the two California redwoods, there was never any doubt that these trees were giants. Early reports of both species described them as dominant in their surroundings, and many estimates of their height or girth or timber content reflected the awesome impression left with a traveller who happened upon these towering groves. One of the first Europeans to see the coast redwoods, the famous botanist and adventurer David Douglas (for whom the Douglas fir is named), called them 'the great beauty of California vegetation . . . which gives the mountains a most peculiar, I was almost going to say awful, appearance.'

California's claim to the world's tallest trees is not entirely undisputed. The only other real contender for this honor, however, is an Australian eucalyptus, which was reported to have specimens 450 feet tall. Extensive research has not validated such claims among living eucalyptus trees, the tallest of which stands 347 feet tall. Another North American tree, the Douglas fir itself, has been measured at 330 feet in height, although its more common stature is near 250 feet, making it the third or fourth in height of all trees. Next in the ranking of tall trees is the other major California redwood, *Sequoiadendron giganteum,* which boasts standing specimens over 300 feet high and is reported to have once grown to a height of 346 feet. One of the Sierra redwood's neighboring trees, the sugar pine, commonly reaches a height of 240 feet.

Other mammoth trees that compete with redwoods for the honor as biggest or tallest include the baobab tree, found in Australia and Africa, which measures up to 60 feet in diameter (not circumference) but grows to a height of only 40 feet, and the kauri pine, of Australia and New Zealand, which claims one specimen of unknown height whose first branch was 80 feet above ground and whose diameter measured 23.8 feet.

With the exception of the kauri pine and eucalyptus, however, all the tallest trees are conifers prized for their straight trunks and excellent timber quality. All these species far outrank the majority of trees in height, as the following brief sampling shows: the ponderosa pine often reaches 200 feet; the longleaf pine and Engelman spruce, both conifers, reach 100 feet in height, as does the nonconiferous sugar maple; and other nonconiferous trees reach less lofty heights—white oak, 75 to 80 feet; paper birch, 65 feet; quaking aspen, 50 feet. The conifers as an order comprise the giants of the tree world, and within that category the redwoods are unmatched in height.

Below: Some of the largest trees reported in botanical literature. Not all their dimensions can be confirmed; one doubtful specimen is the 417-foot Douglas fir.

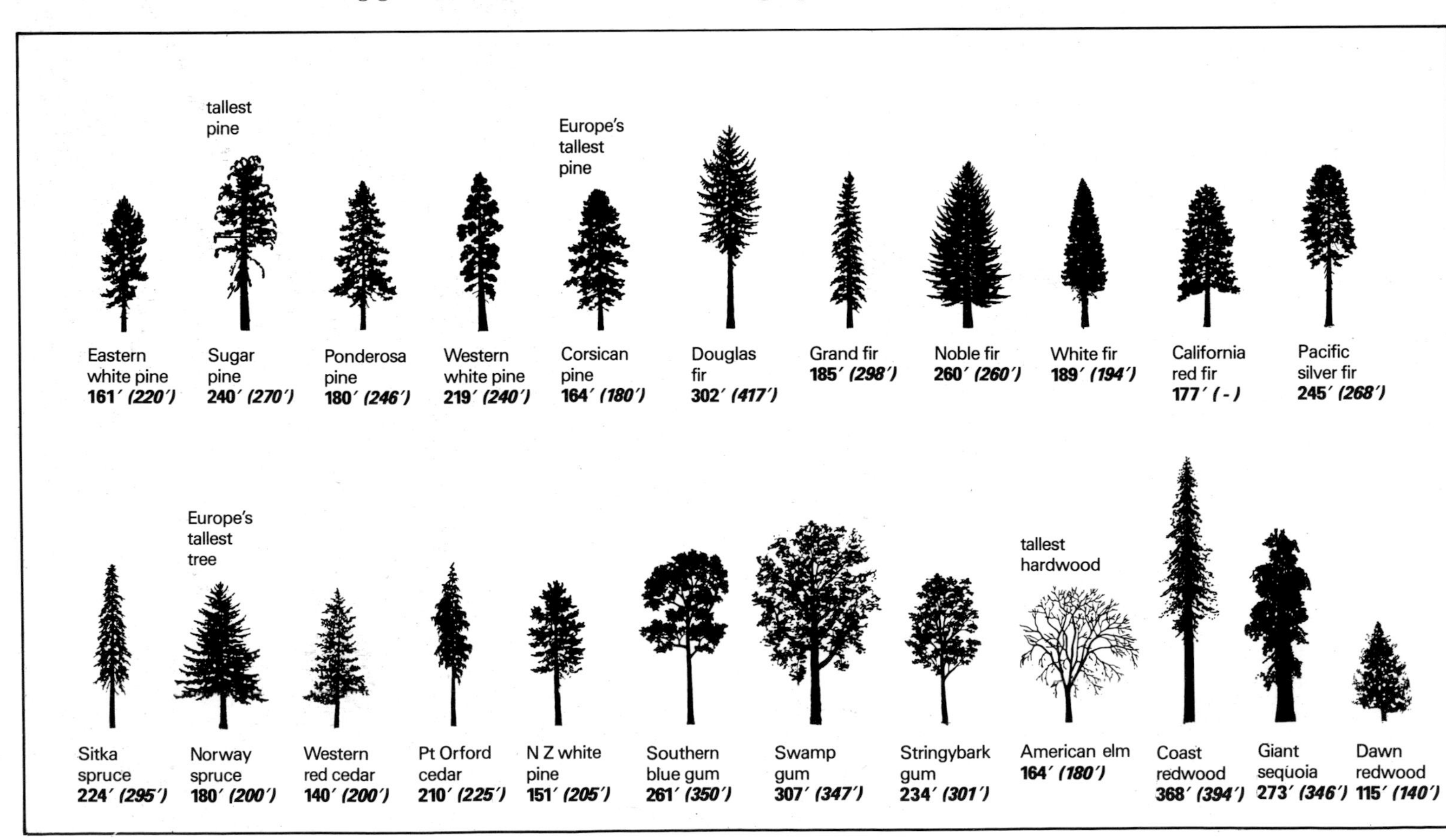

GOD'S OWN FLAGPOLES

Fray Juan Crespi's diary is commonly accepted as the first factual record of the coast redwoods. But a far more tantalizing, if largely unproven, account was written by a Chinese mariner named Hee-li, who navigated the Pacific to Monterey Bay, more than 2000 years before the Spanish saw the redwoods. This Chinese captain ordinarily kept his trading junk close to the Asian coast, his writings state, but a fierce storm blew his ship out to sea in the winter of 217 BC. When the sea had calmed, Hee-li consulted his compass, an unmarked instrument whose needle always pointed south, and sailed for home. What he did not know was that a cockroach had become lodged under the needle, holding it toward the north, so that Hee-li was sailing east when he thought he was heading west. When one of his crew questioned the ship's direction, the captain ordered him thrown overboard. The 10 remaining sailors on Hee-li's junk did not protest, even though they sailed for four months without sighting land. After 125 days, the boat landed on an unfamiliar shore, which Hee-li thought to be an uninhabited part of his own country. Captain and crew explored this new land for several weeks, enjoying the fine weather and marveling at the huge red trees. During this stay, one sailor was assigned to polish the compass, and he discovered the dead cockroach, which he showed to the captain. Hee-li and his crew finally realized that they were four months from their home, and they began preparations for the return voyage. When Hee-li arrived back in China, he wrote an account of the voyage, which was filed in an archive at Si-Ngan-Foo, in the province of Shen-si. The old

Opposite: The sun breaking through the mist and fog in a coastal forest. The large tree on the left is a virgin redwood; this forest also includes young Douglas firs and western azalea shrubs.

manuscript apparently lay undiscovered until an American missionary named Shaw was told the legend of this voyage and in 1890 searched the archives for the lost manuscript. Shaw claimed that he found the account and translated it, and some newspapers carried the story of the missionary's discovery and Hee-li's voyage. Although scholars have questioned the whole story, historians have documented at least some early landings of Chinese vessels on the Pacific Coast of North America. Thus, the Chinese cockroach and the ship's captain Hee-li have joined the lore of the redwoods, which are old enough to have been standing when (and if) the junk put in at Monterey.

Perhaps Hee-li's manuscript will be rediscovered and the tale of the cockroach confirmed one day, but for the present, Spanish missionaries hold claim to informing the Old World about California's magnificent trees. When the northernmost Spanish mission was built at Sonoma in 1823, its founders were living on the threshold of two million acres of virgin coast redwoods. Although the missionaries did not utilize this abundant timber—the missions were built of the traditional adobe brick—the settlers who populated northern California began cutting redwoods for timber in the hills to the east of San Francisco Bay in the 1820s and 1830s. Today, more than 90 percent of those two million acres of trees have been cut, and less than 4 percent of this original virgin forest is protected in state and national parks.

Above: A grouping of burls near the base of a coast redwood tree.

Right: A 'family' of coast redwoods that all sprouted from the same parent tree. Note the woman standing between two of the trunks.

VIRGIN STANDS

The virgin redwoods that remain have changed little since Fray Crespi's visit. *Sequoia sempervirens* is a towering tree, described by one botanist as 'a titan race.' These titans grow from the redwood's seeds, which are so tiny that they measure 123,000 to a pound, or more commonly from a sprout at the base of a tree. The coast redwood is the only conifer that can send vertical sprouts up from the lateral roots lying near the surface of the soil; often as many as a hundred young sprouts will surround an established tree or the stump of a cut or burned tree. It is this pattern of regeneration that results in the characteristic circular grove of this species, in which vertical trunks varying in width from 1 foot to 15 feet soar upward in stately clusters.

Old-growth redwoods in coastal forests commonly reach 300 feet or more in height. At its height of 367.8 feet, the tallest known tree, near Redwood Creek in Redwood National Park, rises higher than a 35-story building. This tree boasts engineering that no manmade structure could match, for it rests on a shallow bed of roots that go no deeper than 6 feet and no wider than 50 feet from its base. Its trunk, or bole, is remarkably straight throughout its upward course, tapering to a pointed spire at the top; the base of the tree is flared, to provide additional support for this lofty expanse. If the tree begins to lean or is damaged at one part of the base, it will grow a buttress to compensate for the added load on one side.

The branches of a virgin coast redwood may begin more than a hundred feet above the forest floor, and the water that travels to the topmost leaves may have to move 400 feet or more to reach them. The leaves of this conifer are of two types: the main shoots carry a spiral arrangement of flat, dark-green needles that point forward; short branchlets have green bracts at the base, above which are larger needles that decrease in size near the tip of the branchlet. When the needles die after three or four years, they do not fall individually; rather, the entire branchlet falls. The soil beneath a cluster of these trees is often blanketed with branchlets, about 1 foot long, still holding neat rows of dead brown needles.

Many branchlets develop cones at their tips. Each of these round cones is ½ inch to 1 inch long and holds 50 to 60 seeds; the cones of an established tree mature in one year and can remain fertile for as long as 15 years. Although they are the secondary means of a coast redwood's reproduction, seeds fall from hanging cones or are released from fallen branchlet cones in huge numbers—one virgin tree is known to have produced five million seeds in a year.

One additional means of regeneration for this tree is the burl, a knoblike growth caused by soil bacteria that often appears on the lower bole. Burls are well known for their unusual patterns of grain and have become valuable as tabletops, clocks and similar decorative items. The burl, too, contains many buds, like the eyes of a potato, which will sprout if the wood is placed in water. If burls are cut through in the lumber-making process and used in timber that is exposed, such as in a train trestle, they will often sprout spontaneously, although the shoots will last only about a year.

Perhaps the most distinctive feature of the coast redwood is its bark. This outer layer, a rich, dark red-brown, gives the tree its name and much of its longevity, by protecting the wood against fires and pests. Redwood bark contains shallow fissures and small ridges in a spongy layer that is 3 to 12 inches thick on mature trees. Both the bark and the tree's heartwood derive their red color from a high content of tannin, a chemical found in many trees; this bitter substance is also one of the tree's agents of protection against insects and fungi.

Above: The coastal range of *Sequoia sempervirens*, which encompasses roughly the northern half of the California coast and two small groves in the southwest corner of Oregon

Above: A coast redwood branchlet, pictured at actual size, showing its round, cypress-type cones and the hard, needlelike leaves similar to those of the fir and hemlock.

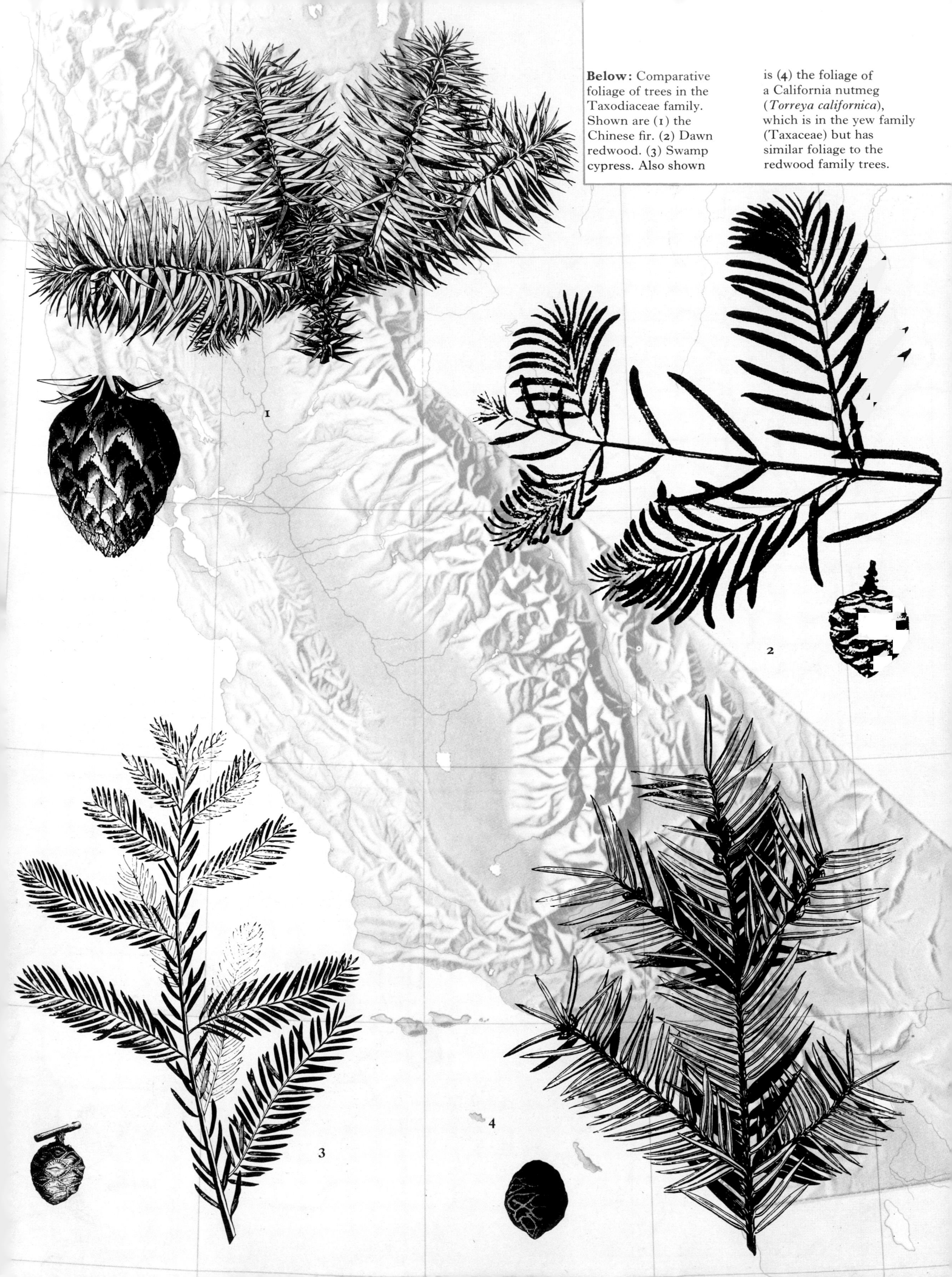

Below: Comparative foliage of trees in the Taxodiaceae family. Shown are (1) the Chinese fir. (2) Dawn redwood. (3) Swamp cypress. Also shown is (4) the foliage of a California nutmeg (*Torreya californica*), which is in the yew family (Taxaceae) but has similar foliage to the redwood family trees.

COASTAL CONDITIONS

ALTHOUGH *Sequoia sempervirens* HAS BEEN CULTIVATED in other areas of the world—including Britain, Europe, Asia, Australia and New Zealand—this tree achieves its majestic heights and lush groupings only in one place. This growth zone is a 450-mile strip along the Pacific Coast, beginning in the southwest corner of Oregon and ending in the Santa Lucia Mountains south of Carmel, California. This band averages 20 miles wide, and the farthest inland these native trees have been found is 40 miles, near a confluence of streams and rivers.

The limiting factor of this relatively small growing area is moisture, which coast redwoods require in great measure. The trees have a close relationship to the largest of oceans, prospering only where winter rains and summer fog maintain an even temperature and a minimum level of moisture. The average rainfall per year in the coastal areas where the world's tallest trees grow is more than 100 inches; in other parts of the growth area, precipitation may be only 20

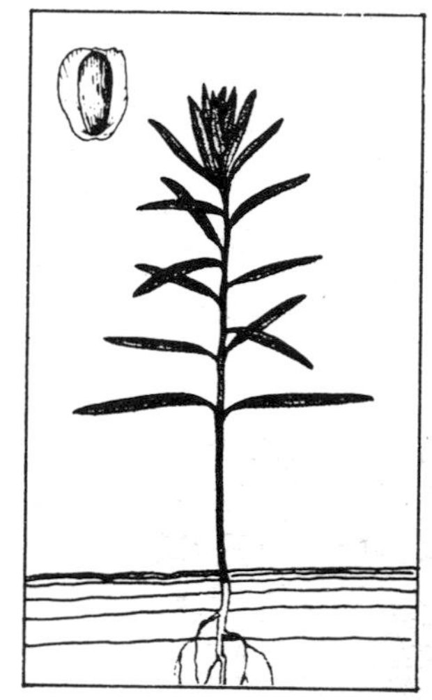

Above: *Sequoia sempervirens* seeds and seedling.

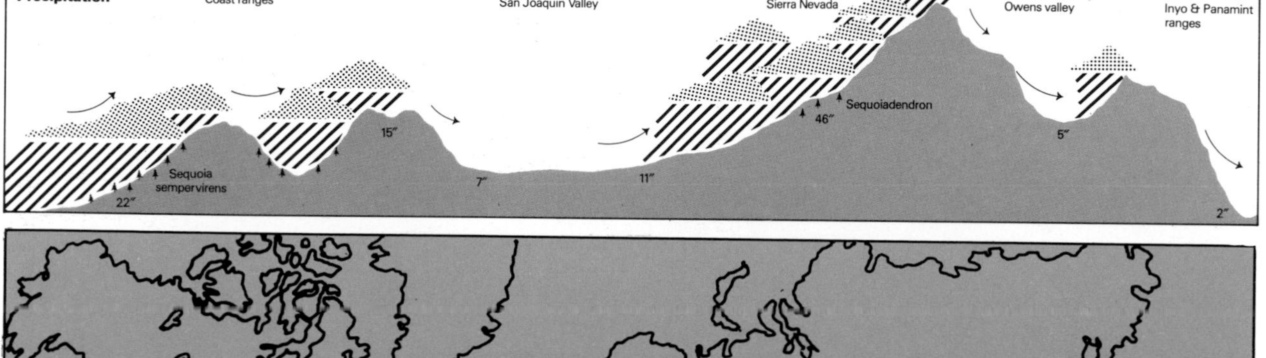

Above left: Typical passage of weather fronts across California from west to east. The distribution of rainfall shows areas that favor growth of the coast and Sierra redwoods.

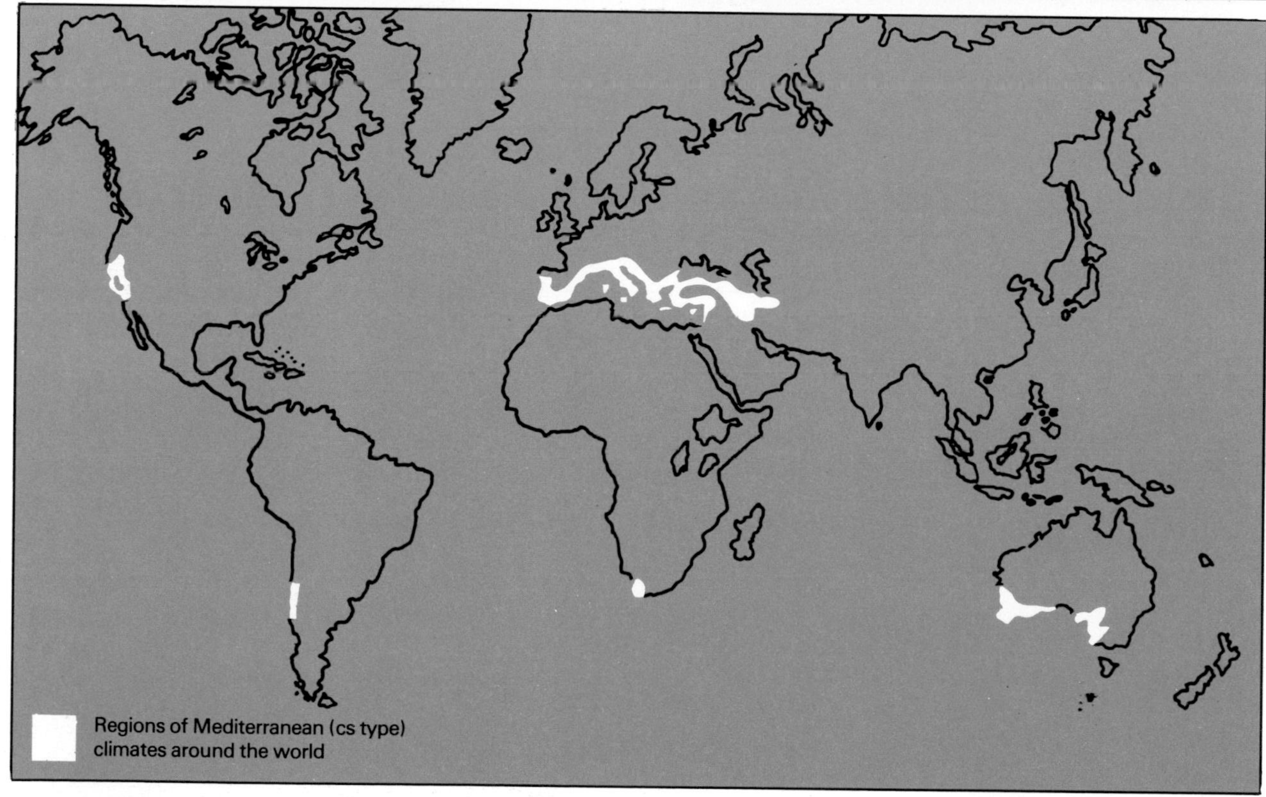

Left: Climates of the world, showing the Mediterranean-type climate where redwoods flourish. This ideal habitat for the two California sequoias exists in very few places on the globe, which explains why these trees reach such majestic proportions only in their native areas.

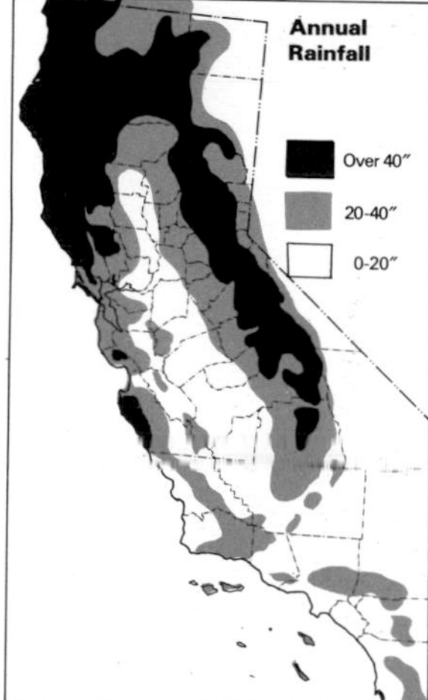

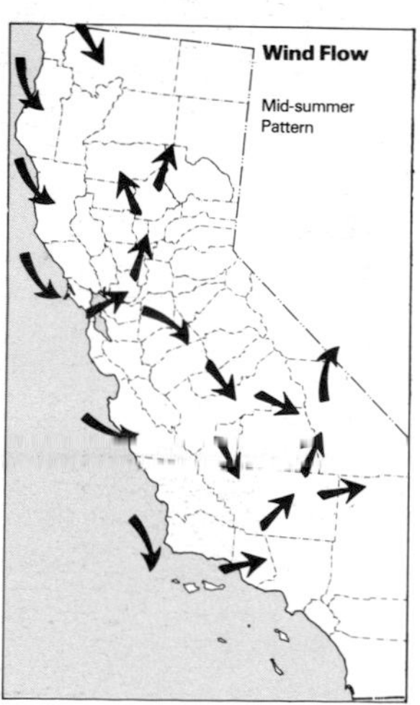

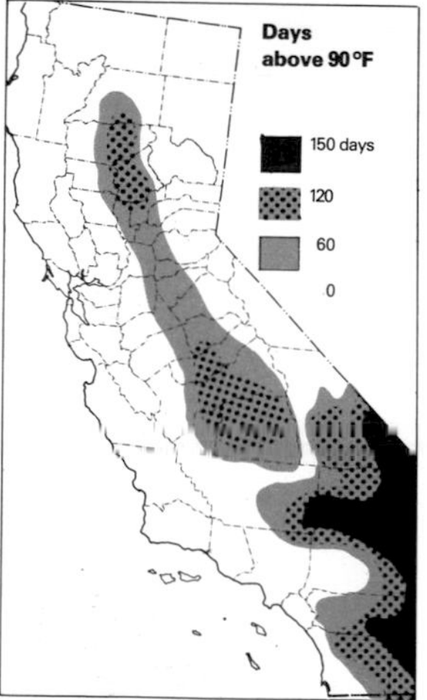

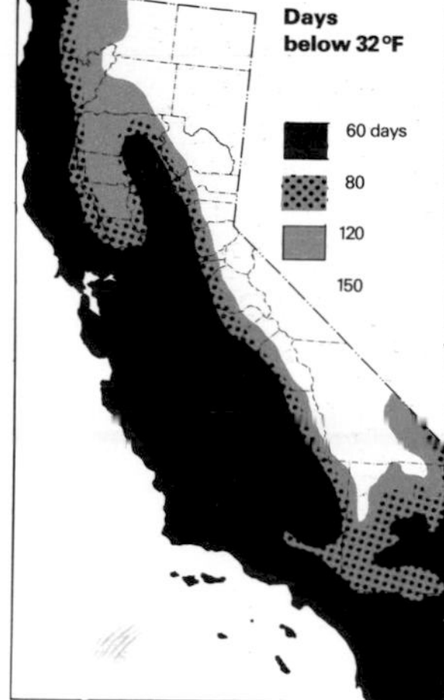

Left: Maps of California, showing rainfall patterns; wind flow patterns; and temperature ranges for summer and winter that the redwoods favor.

Preceding pages: Typical creekside environment in Redwood National Park, showing two common companions of the redwoods, alder trees and sword ferns.

Redwoods: The World's Largest Trees

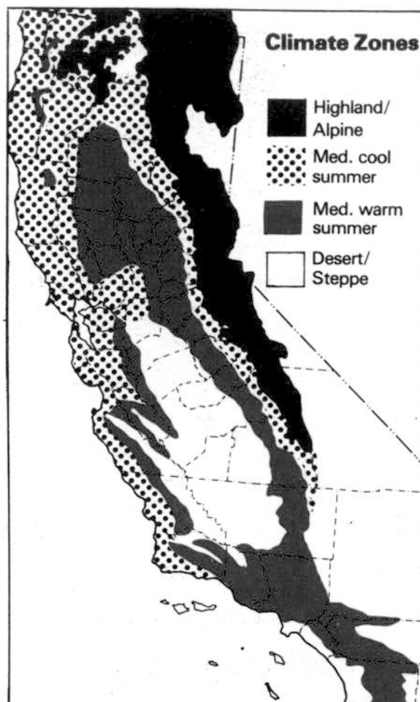

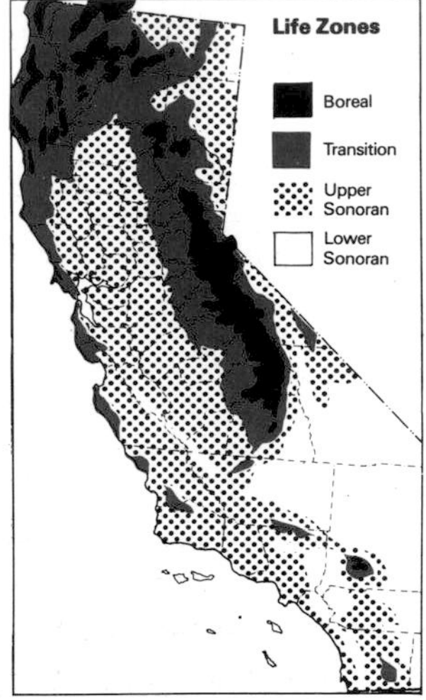

The climate zones of California, showing subdivisions of the Mediterranean-type climate and the vegetation zones of the state. Like most other conifers, both types of redwoods grow in the transitional zone.

to 30 inches per year, although 40 inches is considered the minimum for healthy growth. Temperatures in the redwoods' coastal zone average 44 to 48 degrees Fahrenheit in the coldest months and 60 to 72 degrees in summer and fall, the warmest months. Extreme temperatures in this region rarely go above 100 degrees or below 20 degrees Fahrenheit.

Residents of northern California call this marine-influenced climate 'natural air conditioning,' for the summer fog and winds are drawn inland by the rising heat from the interior valleys of the state. Redwoods thrive in the coastal fog belt, and they help to create their own microclimate within it. Through transpira-

Right: Slope forest, showing a mixture of trees that includes Douglas fir, tan oak, rhododendron and western azalea. This type of mixed growth occurs in canyons and other uneven terrain.

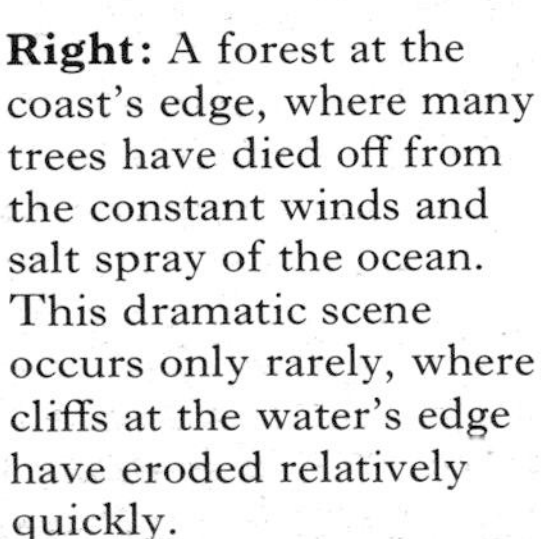

Right: A forest at the coast's edge, where many trees have died off from the constant winds and salt spray of the ocean. This dramatic scene occurs only rarely, where cliffs at the water's edge have eroded relatively quickly.

Far right: Fingers of fog cover the lower elevations of a redwood forest.

tion of moisture from roots to leaves and from leaves into the atmosphere, each coast redwood releases about 500 gallons of water into the air every day. When the coastal fog hits this wall of horizontal precipitation, as it is called, the air's moisture forms into rain. The rain, in turn, resupplies the soil with moisture, and the trees are again nourished. This microclimate is not as dramatic as a tropical rain forest, but the 'rain' in redwood groves—which is often a morning and evening drip from the trees, rather than a real shower—keeps the atmosphere cool and damp at most times.

Although the ocean's moisture and winds are essential to the coast redwoods' growth, these trees do not prosper at the edge of the Pacific. The salt spray of waves and winds on the coast damages young redwoods, and the often heavy winds are too forceful for the shallow-rooted trees. The tallest specimens grow at low elevations and in close proximity to streams, and no native coast redwoods grow at elevations above 3000 feet.

The large groupings of virgin trees are often called 'flat' stands, because of their location in the flat terraces along streams and rivers and because these long-standing groves contain many trees of the same towering height, giving the forest an appearance of evenness. Though celebrated and spectacular, these flat stands occupy only about 2 percent of the existing coast redwood forest.

Left: A flat stand of even-age, old-growth coast redwoods, showing a predominance of large trees of similar size. The world's tallest trees are found in flat stands, which flourish on level ground near streams.

A second type of coastal forest is called 'slope' growth, for it covers the uneven terrain of upper streambeds and canyons. This kind of forest is more mixed than the flat growth, containing trees of varied sizes and a larger array of associated plants, such as rhododendron, huckleberry, oxalis and wild iris. Other types of trees have a greater opportunity to grow in slope forest, because the area is not dominated by the persistent shade of huge virgin groves; among the slope trees that prosper with redwoods are the western maple and the silver fir.

Left: Bolling Memorial Grove in Big Basin State Park. This first state park in California is in the southern part of the coast redwoods' range.

STRONG SURVIVORS

THE PRINCIPAL REASON THAT VIRGIN COAST REDWOODS have lived for 2000 years or more is that only the most radical assaults can kill them. Until the northern California coast was settled and heavily logged in the 1850s, the only threats to these trees were fire and climatic change. From the evidence of trees that have stood for more than 20 centuries, and from geologic research, only the subtlest of climatic alterations have taken place since the glaciers withdrew before reaching this favored coastal territory.

Temporary changes, such as drought or unseasonal cold, can damage the tallest trees by affecting their supply of moisture. Every old-growth forest (one containing a high percentage of virgin trees) contains a few 'spike-tops,' trees that are dead at the highest part of the trunk but are green and healthy below. Usually the cause of this partial death is moisture stress, or an inability of the tree to supply enough water to the topmost leaves and branches.

Fire has been a more persistent threat to the coast redwoods, but only the greatest conflagrations could kill the old-growth trees. Many of these trees bear fire scars that have damaged their boles and left their bases hollow, but the great trees were not toppled and their growth

Opposite: Richly patterned bark near the base of an old-growth coast redwood.

Right: Dramatic view of a fire scar on a *Sequoia sempervirens*.

Below: Rare view of snow in a coast redwood grove testifies to these trees' ability to withstand temporary extremes of climate. Very young redwoods, however, would be damaged or killed by freezing temperatures.

continued without interruption.

The periodic wildfires that are commonly a part of natural forest life tend to favor the continued dominance of virgin stands, as well as the germination of new sprouts and seedlings. Because of its thick protective bark and its lack of resin (a flammable substance that most trees contain), the coast redwood often remains standing when other species of trees are consumed in a forest fire. In trees that have sustained significant damage, the ability to sprout from the trunk also keeps redwoods growing. New sprouts also come from the fire-blackened areas of a partially burned tree; this new growth is called a fire column for the pattern of growth along the flames' precise route.

These trees' dominance in a mixed forest is augmented by the boost that a ground fire gives to redwood seeds. Ordinarily the tiny seeds of *Sequoia sempervirens* cannot penetrate the thick organic matter on the forest floor—the carpet of fallen branchlets and decaying ferns and ground cover keep them from reaching the soil in which they could grow. This organic matter also contains a fungus that preys on the roots of redwood seedlings, further imperilling these trees at their one truly fragile stage. When a wildfire sweeps through the forest, however, it consumes the organic matter and sterilizes the soil of this fungus. Thus, seeds falling on the newly exposed soil have a greater chance to germinate and prosper.

Besides occasional wildfires, periodic flooding of the many streams and rivers in the terrain is another characteristic of the coast redwood's growth belt. Just as the trees are largely impervious to fire, so can they withstand both floods and the ensuing deposits of silt that often kill other trees. For most species, if the soil level becomes too high on a tree's trunk, the roots begin to rot—in effect, the tree is smothered. Because of their great height and shallow roots, however, the coast redwoods can accommodate flood conditions much more easily than their forest companions.

These trees also have a unique ability to generate a vertical root through soil newly deposited by flooding and then to create a new lateral root system at this higher level, effectively maintaining their shallow support at the necessary depth of 4 to 6 feet. One fallen tree, studied by a University of California forestry expert, bore soil marks and old roots that proved it had begun life on a forest floor that was 11 feet lower than the one where it fell. However, owing to this characteristic shallowness, the root system cannot always hold a huge tree in place during a major flood, and many virgin trees have been toppled by the combined effects of their water-weighted tops and torrents at their bases.

Two other special characteristics of the coast redwood contribute to its longevity. The tree's armor of thick bark and tannin content make it largely invulnerable to pests; one beetle and two types of fungi are commonly found in association with the tree, but none of these invaders can kill it. The other favorable trait that is unique to this conifer is its ability to regenerate from a stump or fallen tree. Whole groves of second-growth redwoods surround many virgin remnants, and a flood- or wind-fallen tree may send up hundreds of new sprouts all along it bole.

Left: Drawing of the male and female parts of the coast redwood. At the time of pollination, wind blows pollen from the male cones (right) to the female cones (left), where the sperm from the male cone fertilizes the female egg. The female cone then matures into the round cone that produces the tree's seeds.

Above: The redwood cone at progressive stages of development, concluding with the release of seeds.

Opposite: Sunlight reaches young trees among the old-growth redwoods, encouraging perpetuation of this forest.

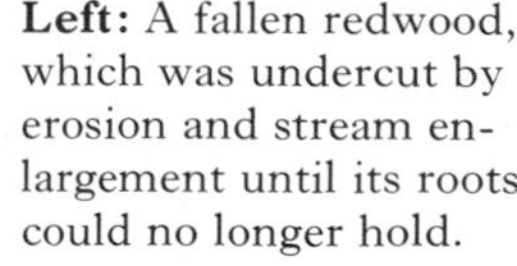

Left: A fallen redwood, which was undercut by erosion and stream enlargement until its roots could no longer hold.

NATURE'S ADAPTATIONS

These uncommonly hardy trees are able to adapt to genetic mutations and environmental changes. One fascinating form of alteration is the albino coast redwood, in which a gene mutation causes the tree to have white leaves. This comparatively delicate plant cannot manufacture its own food, because it lacks chlorophyll, and thus it lives like a parasite, deriving all nourishment from the parent tree from which it has sprouted.

Because it lacks chlorophyll in its leaves, the albino tree employs a modified version of transpiration to obtain both food and water from green trees. In a normal tree, the top of a leaf contains only a few pores, and the water released during transpiration and photosynthesis is sent through the many openings in the leaf's underside. Albino leaves, however, contain numerous pores in the upper side as well as the lower, which increases the plant's capacity for transpiration. While this ability to move larger quantities of water and nutrients into the leaves is the albino's mechanism for staying alive, the greater number of surface pores also makes the plant more susceptible to damage when exposed to extreme temperatures. Ordinary green leaves can close their surface pores during periods of high heat—generally above 80 degrees Fahrenheit—or at temperatures below freezing. The more numerous pores of the albino's leaf make this protective maneuver more difficult, and if a 'shutdown' is necessary for prolonged periods, an albino plant might fail to gain nourishment through transpiration and thus could wither and die.

Occasionally an albino redwood stands alone in the forest, but it is connected by an extensive root system to a conventional green relative nearby. Most often these white redwoods are found at the base of one or more large trees, and their foliage contains both arresting white-needled branches and a number of dead brown areas. The tallest specimens of albino coast redwood measure 50 to 60 feet (although one of 84 feet was 'topped' for a Christmas tree by some thoughtless person recently), but these 'ghosts of the forest' usually grow no taller than 15 feet.

These striking albino mutants are quite rare in coastal forests, and their tendency to nestle among larger trees' trunks makes them very difficult to find. The largest and oldest albino redwoods—some estimated at 150 years of age—are hidden in the deep forests, away from most roads or trails. Two smaller specimens are

Above and right: Three examples of albino coast redwood trees, which contain no chlorophyll and thus cannot manufacture food. Albinos are relatively rare specimens, always found on or near thriving green trees on which the albinos depend for nourishment.

easily reached, however; one is flourishing between two trees beside the main trail in Muir Woods, near San Francisco, and another fair-sized albino stands beside the entrance to a public campground in Big Sur, south of Carmel, California. Curiously, the albinos' distribution pattern seems to contrast with that of its green forebears; the largest and tallest green redwoods are concentrated in the northern end of the coastal growing area, while the known albinos are more numerous in the southern part of this range. Scientists have begun a program of grafting and propagating these unusual specimens, so albino redwoods may eventually be cultivated as decorative trees outside their coastal forests.

Another adaptation of the coast redwood has been imposed on the trees by a flock of birds. In one small area of the California coast, about 20 miles north of San Francisco, great blue herons and great egrets have been nesting in a grove of redwoods for a century. These large birds, about 5 feet tall and with wingspreads of 4 to 5 feet, long ago selected the shallow, sheltered feeding ground of Bolinas Lagoon as their spring breeding area, and the steep-walled canyon behind this lagoon became the site for their nests. One stand of second-growth redwoods was the ideal choice from among the available trees, and it is here that the birds perch 100 feet up in shaky-looking nests made of sticks.

Over the last hundred years, the nesting of the herons and egrets has resulted in a flat-topped redwood grove—not a genetic mutation, of course, but a permanent alteration of more than 100 trees. Each winter 180 egrets and 100 herons return to this canyon home, carrying on courtship and nest building in a raucous fashion.

Above: Young herons in a nest at the top of a truncated redwood in Audubon Canyon Ranch in northern California.

Left: Painting of a mating pair of egrets in their redwood eyrie, also at Audubon Canyon Ranch, where for many generations these shore birds have wintered and raised their young.

These birds are uninvited gardeners for the coast redwood grove, for in their annual nest construction the birds pull the uppermost branches off the trees. Over the century since the shore birds established their rookery in the trees, the tops of these redwoods have been been transformed from graceful pointed spires to truncated platforms of living branches and dead sticks, all woven into a precarious-looking network of 140 crowded nests.

Each pair of herons and egrets shares the incubation and food-gathering duties, tending to as many as five eggs and nestlings. The baby birds cannot fly for the first seven to nine weeks of life, so from April to June the redwood rookery is a noisy center of bustling birds ferrying food from the lagoon and of demanding chicks calling for nourishment. By midsummer the young birds have mastered the art of flying and fishing, and they join the flocks to fly to winter homes in warm areas of North America, Mexico and Central America.

Like many other unique natural areas, the heron and egret rookery in northern California was almost lost to 'progress.' Since the hillsides were originally logged in the 1860s, the rookery had been part of a 506-acre dairy ranch and had remained undisturbed. In 1955 a private realtor purchased the ranch, intending to subdivide the property for recreational housing. In response, the local Audubon Society mounted a campaign to save the property from development, which would have certainly threatened the nesting and feeding sanctuary of these birds. The conservation group was able to buy the ranch in 1961, and its campaign to forestall commercial development of the lagoon and a neighboring island succeeded. Today the odd-looking redwoods and their unlikely inhabitants are the principal attractions at Audubon Canyon Ranch.

Nature's more abrupt alterations of some redwood trees have provided sanctuary for other forest dwellers. The hollow butts of coast redwoods that were damaged by fire have served as shelter for travellers, including famed explorer John C Fremont, and once were makshift homes for coast Indians. One such tree in a virgin grove has a 4-foot opening inside its base, and a large part of the trunk is supported by a rim of solid growth only 20 inches thick. Such open-based trees were called 'goosepens' by early settlers and loggers, reputedly because some farmers kept flocks of geese inside them. One pack-train operator is supposed to have corraled his 33 pack mules in such a hollow tree, and enterprising moonshiners set up whiskey stills in these obscure locations during Prohibition in the 1920s.

Above: Big Basin forest, an early treehouse in an old hollow redwood.

Right: A 'corkscrew tree,' named for its unusual twisting pattern of growth, located near the Redwood Highway north of Orrick.

Below: An exposed redwood on a bluff above the Pacific. Branches cover most of the trunk in this weather-washed specimen, whose location prevents its full, normal development.

A TYPICAL WATERSHED

1▲

2▲

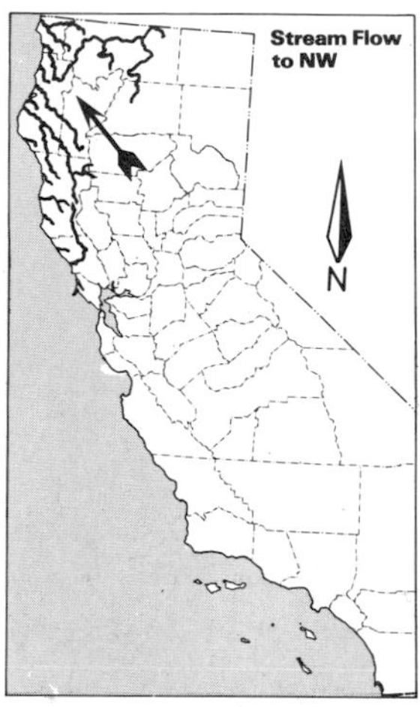

Left: Views from several areas of coast redwood watersheds, shown in progressive order from farthest inland to nearest the coast. These coastal river valleys consistently run southeast to northwest. (1) A rivulet near its source far from the coast. (2) A wider stream with large redwoods beside it. (3) A flat area where the creek is slow-moving and wide—the likely site of flooding. (4) A natural lagoon, still many miles inland from the coast. (5) A manmade dam on a redwood forest creek.

4▼

3▲

5▼

Redwoods: The World's Largest Trees

Watershed views midway from the creek's source to the ocean. (1) The dark area in this infrared aerial view is a manmade lake. The white patches in the photo are sites of clearcut logging. (2) A hill where a typical clearcut has been made. (3) A flat creek area where sediment has collected, much of it from erosion caused by logging activity. (4) An inland valley that has been cleared for farming. (5) A ranch among the coastal redwood forest, where stumps of cut trees still dot the pastures.

1▲ 2▲ 3▲ 4▲ 5▼

6▲

7▲

8▲

9▲

11▼

10▲

12▼

Watershed views approaching the coast. (6) Foggy hills that were logged selectively, note where new growth has taken hold. (7) A damaged watershed of a tributary stream—logging and erosion have prevented new growth on the steep banks. (8) An example of the massive deposits of silt from logging erosion and winter storm runoff, which cover more of the creekbed than the creek itself. (9) A wall along the creek's bank that was washed out by a flood. A flat stand of redwoods along the creek's bottomland, in an area that has not been damaged by flood or silt deposits. (10) The grove of virgin trees on Redwood Creek that contains the world's tallest tree. (11) The mouth of a creek in the northern California redwood region. (12) The placid waters and dunes of the estuary where fresh water meets the Pacific.

THE REDWOOD FOREST

The renowned German architect Eric Mendelsohn is said to have called the coast redwoods 'God's own flagpoles' upon seeing them for the first time in Muir Woods. His description is a fitting one, for these tall, straight trees rise higher than any living thing, and their sheltering groves have inspired many comparisons with cathedrals. The immensity of these redwood spires is made all the more profound by their number; a virgin stand can contain dozens of trees that reach 300 feet or more in height.

Although coast redwoods dominate their surroundings with lofty crowns and thick groves that combine to shade most of the forest floor, their environment is rich with other plants and a variety of animals. The extremely wet areas in the northernmost part of the redwoods' coastal range are particularly dense with lush undergrowth. Ferns thrive in this continuous moisture; the common varieties at the redwoods' bases include sword fern, five-finger fern, deer fern, licorice fern and maidenhair fern.

Ferns of the redwood forest.

Lady fern

Coast wood fern

Western sword fern

Giant chain fern.

The small flowering plants that cover the moist ground in many places include oxalis (also called redwood sorrel), alum root, wild ginger and bleeding heart. Often these thick populations of plants cover a dozen acres or more, forming a carpet of delicate colors around the red-brown trunks. Flowering shrubs and berries, including a variety of dogwood, California huckleberry, azalea and rhododendron, also populate the redwoods' domain. A less welcome member of this community is poison oak, which often climbs high on the redwood trunks.

The diversity of trees that share the coastal forest with redwoods is impressive as well. The three most common species are quite different from each other: Douglas fir, the tall and valuable timber tree; tan oak, an aggressive tree that crowds other plants out of its path to sunlight; and madrone (often called arbutus), a red-limbed tree that also prefers sun to shade. Two other oaks, the Oregon and the black, also inhabit the warmer and higher redwood areas. Near streams, the big-leaf maple and red alder can be found, and on the ocean side of the redwood growth range, four conifers share the territory—coast hemlock, Sitka spruce, lowland fir and Port Orford cedar.

Such a rich forest terrain invites many animals, even though most of them are shy of casual human visitors. Two of the most skittish inhabitants of this environment are the bobcat and the black bear, which hunt at night and can usually be traced only by their tracks. A herd of elk thrives in Prairie Creek Redwood State Park, and deer are numerous in all the coastal forests. Squirrels live in the branches of redwoods, and raccoons prowl the forest floor and trees, often raiding the treetop nests of egrets and herons in the coastside rookery at Audubon Canyon. In addition to these shore birds, more than a hundred other avian species are common to the coastal forests and waters.

The varied mixture of trees and plants of all sizes and ages in the old-growth redwood forest represents a 'climax community,' the natural balance of plant species that has been attained over centuries. If left undisturbed by human intervention or natural catastrophe, such complex ecosystems will sustain their healthy composition indefinitely. Examples of climax communities are rare, particularly in such populous places as California; thus, protection for them is all the more important, for they are easily accessible displays of nature in its purest form.

The exact time at which any given virgin redwood forest reached climax balance has not been charted, but it is known that the California coastal groves had achieved this status before the rush of settlements and logging camps in the 1850s. These self-perpetuating environments may have been fully developed for a thousand years ago or more, since the oldest specimens of *Sequoia sempervirens,* their dominant species, have been growing for 2200 years. The redwoods' longevity and the survival of these climax communities have also saved from extinction many of their associated forest plants.

1▲

2▲

3▼

◄4

Flora and fauna of the coastal forest. (1) Raccoons in the cleft of a redwood trunk. (2) The cougar, a seldom-seen resident of the area. (3) The spotted owl, another scarcely glimpsed forest dweller. (4) A pair of Roosevelt elk in Prairie Creek Redwoods State Park.

1▲

2▲

Flora and fauna of the coastal forest: (1) Unusual fungus growing on a fallen redwood log. (2) A young Santa Cruz garter snake. (3) Redwood sorrel (oxalis) on the forest floor. (4) The wild, delicate Douglas iris. (5) The striking fern canyon of Prairie Creek State Park. (6) The bobcat, an elusive resident of the redwood region.

3▲

4▲

5▼

6

7▲

8▲

9▲

10▲

11▲

12▲

13▼

14▼

15

(7) Merriam's chipmunk. (8) Mature cones and foliage of *Sequoia sempervirens*. (9) Western bracken at the base of a redwood. (10) A young rabbit taking cover on the forest floor. (11) A mule deer in a forest meadow. (12) The noisy Steller's jay. (13) The western salamander. (14) A tan oak at the edge of a stand of redwoods. (15) The ubiquitous raccoon.

THE HISTORY TOLD BY TREES

Because of its growth rings and its many centuries of life, a coast redwood can provide a sort of map of history. In 1934 Professor Emanuel Fritz, of the University of California, made a detailed study of a fallen redwood in Richardson Grove State Park, in Humboldt County, that plots the major events in its 1204-year life. This 310-foot tree fell in 1933, finally giving in to the 40-foot lean that had developed after its roots were damaged by fire on one side. Much of this tree's history holds clues to the life of a forest that few men ever saw.

In making his study, which is now a permanent exhibit on the site in Richardson Grove, Fritz carefully exposed the tree's root system and had the trunk sawn through to reveal the rings and other interior marks. This evidence shows that the tree survived at least nine fires, the first in 1147 and subsequent major blazes in 1595, 1789 and 1806. In 1820 a near-killing fire hit this tree, burning through the bark and cambium and into the heartwood on one side.

Right: The exposed root system of a fallen coast redwood; note the partially exposed trunk section outlined in white. This is the tree studied by Emanuel Fritz.

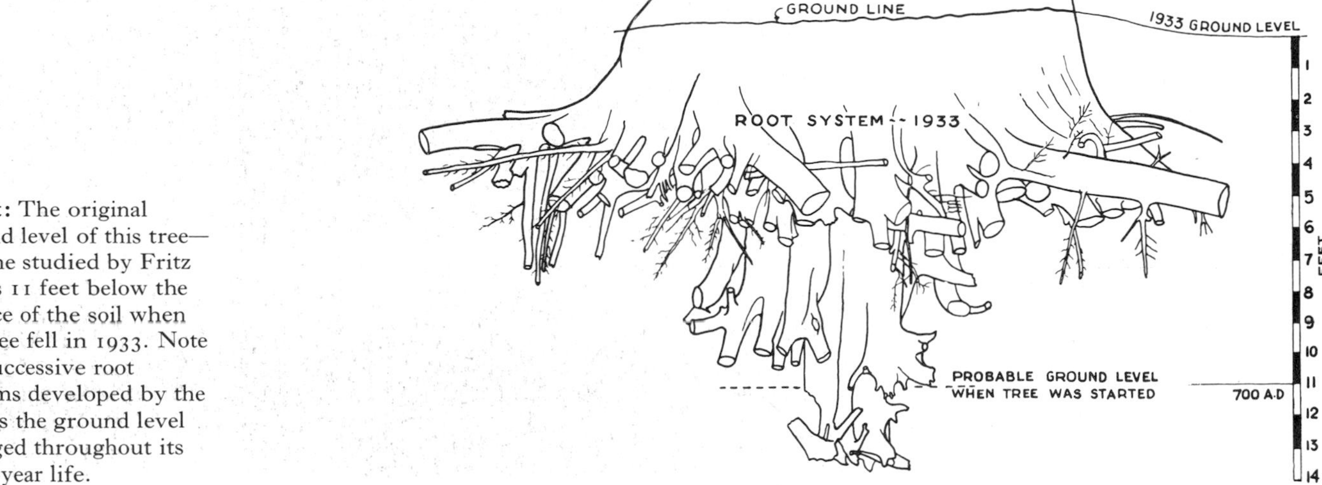

Right: The original ground level of this tree—the one studied by Fritz—was 11 feet below the surface of the soil when the tree fell in 1933. Note the successive root systems developed by the tree as the ground level changed throughout its 1200-year life.

Left: Cross-section of the fallen tree showing the major points in its history. This redwood lived from about the year 700 to 1933.

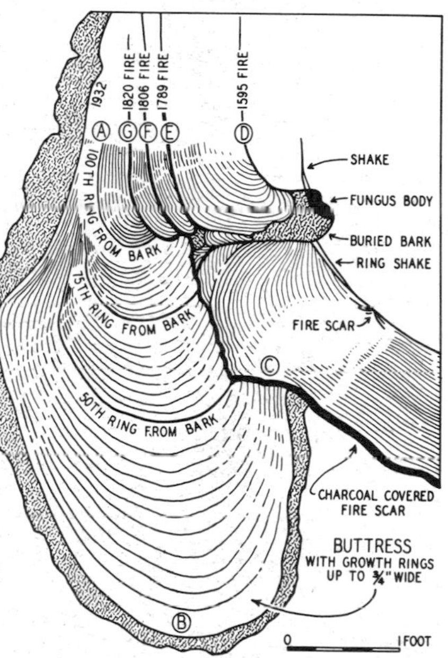

Left: Good view of the buttress that this tree grew after fire damage; this extra growth added strength and compensated for the lost trunk area through several successive fires.

Approximately 40 percent of the tree's circumference was dead after the 1820 fire, but the tree had already begun to form a buttress in response to previous fire damage, and the buttress growth quickened and somehow supplied enough support to keep the tree upright, though leaning. Fritz's examination of the roots and stump also revealed that this tree had withstood seven major floods in a thousand years.

The fact that this tree survived seven floods and nine fires and continued growing with nearly half its trunk surface burned away is clear testimony to the strength and endurance of the coast redwood. Additionally, that the tree's partially damaged root system supported a tree that weighed one million pounds for 113 years after it began caving in is almost beyond comprehension. In short, the history of this one indomitable tree seems equal to any tale a pioneer could tell, and worthy of the humble respect of mere humans.

Left: The 'Shrine Tree' along Redwood Highway in northern California; the fire scar has been enlarged to add drama to this tourist attraction, which is not really 5000 years old—its age is probably no more than 2000 years.

MOTHERS OF THE FOREST

California's other redwood, *Sequoiadendron giganteum,* is probably the more famous of the two trees but the less well known as a species of redwood. The giant sequoias of the Sierra Nevada are so massive that they seem an almost outlandish phenomenon of nature. From the earliest reports of the Big Trees, the certainty of their place as the largest living things has not been seriously questioned.

The first record of discovery of giant sequoias was made by Zenas Leonard, one of 40 men who crossed the Nevada desert and Sierra mountains on an exploratory trip to California led by Joseph Walker. In 1833 this group passed through a grove of Big Trees, which later research determined to be either the Merced or the Tuolumne grove, but did not stay because winter was approaching and the area lacked food. Leonard kept a diary of the expedition, however, noting that they 'found some trees of the redwood species, incredibly large . . .' which he estimated at 16 to 18 fathoms (96 to 108 feet) in circumference. Leonard published his account of this journey in 1839, but apparently his story did not attract any significant interest, probably because the small book was published in Pennsylvania.

It was not until 1852 that the Big Trees received the notoriety that would become their hallmark for a generation or more. The Gold Rush had brought a mining boom to the Sierra region, and one beneficiary of this growth was the Union Water Company of Murphy's Camp, which was constructing a canal for water supplies in the area. A local hunter, A T Dowd, was hired by the company to live with the workmen and shoot game for their food. One

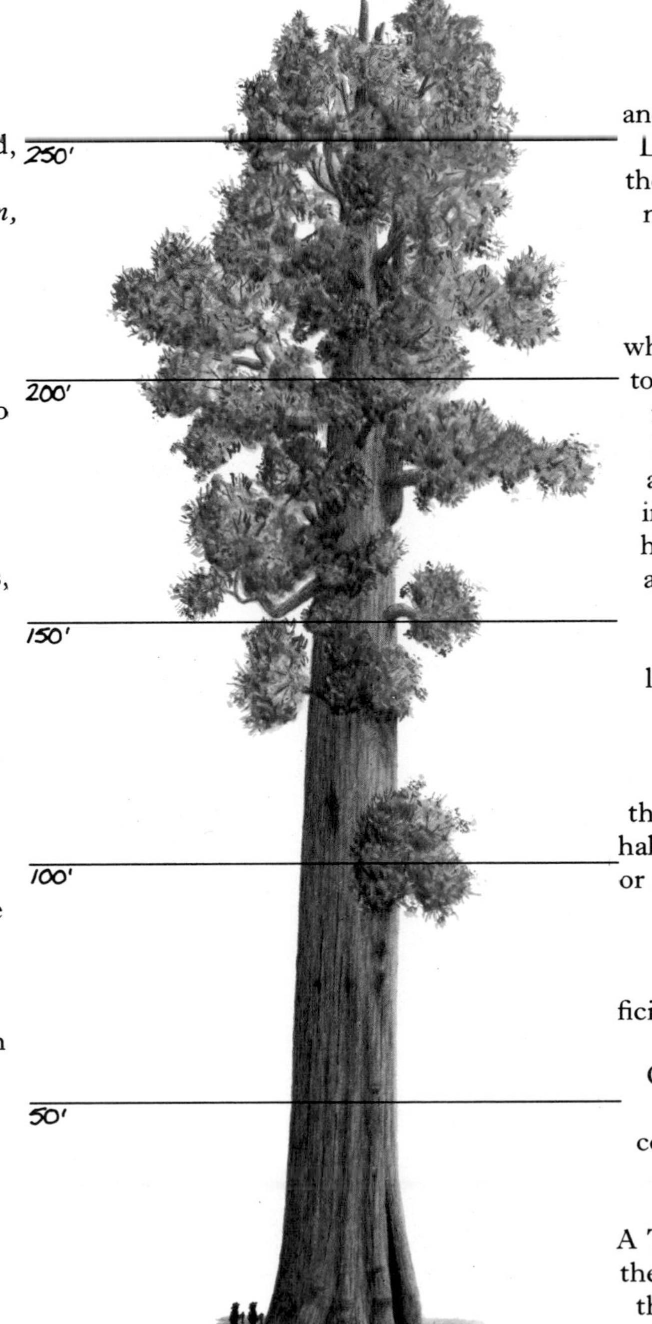

Opposite: Snow and fog among the giant sequoias of the Giant Forest in Sequoia National Park.

day Dowd wounded a grizzly bear and chased it through the forest for a long distance before losing track of the animal. In the course of his pursuit, the hunter encountered the largest tree he had ever seen, and when he returned to the construction camp he described his discovery to the workmen. The others would not believe Dowd's story, calling it his 'big tree yarn' and making a joke of the episode.

Several days later, on a Sunday morning, Dowd again went out to look for game and returned to camp breathless and excited. He reported that he had just shot the biggest grizzly he had ever seen, and he would need the help of all the men in camp to bring it back. Since it was Sunday, the men were not working, and most of the construction crew accompanied Dowd through several miles of backwoods and canyons to the place where the hunter had first seen the giant sequoia. Dowd pointed to the tree and said, 'This is the large grizzly I was talking about.' The other woodsmen were as

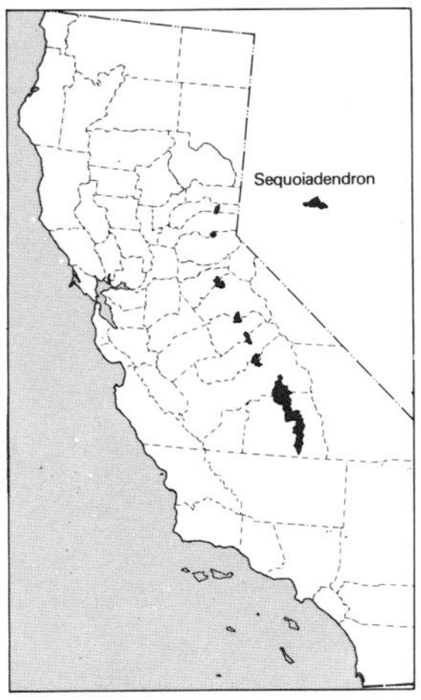

Above: The range of growth of the giant sequoia in California.

Right: The massive domes of the giant sequoia are just visible behind the sugar pines and white firs in the foreground, as seen in an 1850s illustration.

amazed by their find as Dowd had been, and instead of chastising him for his deception, they explored the area and found many more huge trees, then carried the word of their discovery of the trees known as Calaveras Grove, located in Calaveras County, back to civilization.

A newspaper article in the Sonora *Herald*, in June 1852, told Dowd's story in print, and within a few months word of the Big Trees had spread across the United States and Europe. When the news reached the public, a number of other adventurers came forward to claim that they had actually discovered the giant trees years before. One Californian, John Bidwell, reported that he had gone on a hunting trip as a boy in 1841 and happened upon a grove of such trees. Three other local men claimed that they had carved their initials in the burned part of a tree in the Calaveras Grove in 1850, and a later newspaper account stated that the carving had been located. Still other writers have given credit for the discovery of the Big Trees to such far-flung adventurers as the Prince of Weid, in Germany, who supposedly saw the trees sometime between 1832 and 1834, and an Irishman, John Barrington, who reported sending seeds of giant sequoia to his father in Ireland in 1844. Various botanical sources state that seeds from these trees were in propagation in Europe before the celebrated Dowd discovery.

As noted earlier the Sierra redwood had almost as many proposed names as it had discoverers. Nevertheless, as the international naming feud proceeded, exploration and location of Sierra redwood groves went on in the mountains. The last of the immense groves was found in 1933, making a total of 35,607 acres of Big Trees in 75 groves. The Big Tree range covers a 260-mile-long area that is at most 15 miles wide. All the groves are located on the western slope of the Sierra Nevada, at elevations between 4500 and 7500 feet. The vast majority of giant sequoias are concentrated in the southern part of this range; only seven major groves are north of Fresno County, and these are widely separated from each other.

Unlike the coast redwoods, which have a larger range and are still cut from commercial timberlands, the giant sequoias are virtually all in public ownership. A scant 8 percent of the trees are held on private lands, with the balance divided as follows: 68 percent in national parks; 21 percent in national forests; 2 percent in state or county ownership; and 1 percent belonging to the federal Bureau of Indian Affairs.

Below: Distribution of trees on the slopes of the Sierra Nevada Mountains. The giant sequoia grows in the moist area between 4500 and 7500 feet on the western elevation.

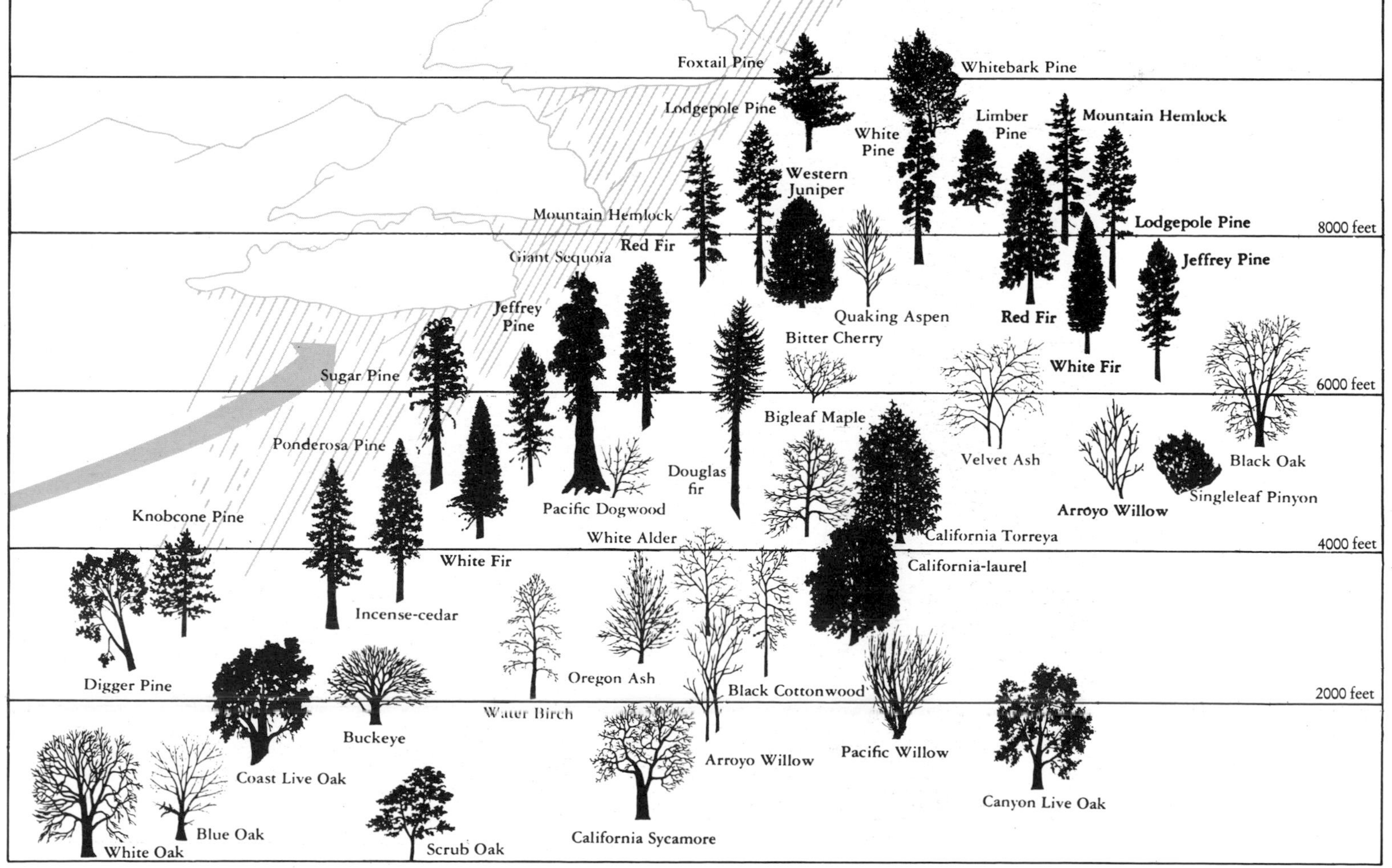

GROVES AMONG THE MOUNTAINS

Opposite: Snow-dusted giant sequoia in Round Meadow of Sequoia National Park.

DESPITE THEIR ENORMOUS SIZE, Sierra redwoods are limited to areas with specific growing conditions. These trees require moist, sandy soil and adequate warmth and precipitation, which effectively halts their expansion beyond the established groves—the areas to the south are too arid and the areas to the north are too cold. Big Trees flourish under conditions of 45 to 60 inches of precipitation each year, which is provided by winter snow melt and spring rain. These trees can stand temperatures of 0 degrees Fahrenheit and will tolerate several feet of snow during the winter so long as the summer provides adequate sunshine for renewed growth.

The tree that rises from a tiny seed—giant sequoias do not sprout from the base as their coastal relatives can—is imposing indeed. Its height averages 200 to 250 feet, with a few old-growth trees reaching 300 feet or more. The tree gets its name from its bulk, however; the diameters of giant sequoias vary between 15 feet, for a tree in relatively dry soil, to 30 feet, for one in ideal growing conditions. Amazingly, the Sierra redwood's trunk does not taper to any degree from the top of its spreading base to the crown of the tree. Comparative measurements made in 1932 of the two largest giant sequoias showed that the mean diameter of the largest tree decreased only $\frac{1}{2}$ foot in 60 feet of growth; the diameter was 17.5 feet at a height of 60 feet and 17.0 feet at a height of 120 feet. The second largest tree tapered slightly more, measuring 16.3 feet in diameter at 60 feet high and 15.0 feet at 120 feet high. The fact that limbs on such old and large specimens begin about a hundred feet off the ground simply adds to the observer's sense of the trees' imposing mass.

The base of a Sierra redwood broadens to almost twice the width of the trunk proper to support the tree's enormous weight and height. The diameter of the two largest trees at their bases is 34.3 feet and 35.7 feet, respectively. (The second largest tree has a wider base but does not have the total volume of the largest one.) Very often the base of a large sequoia is buttressed, to compensate for soil erosion on one side or damage to the trunk or roots, usually from fire.

The root system of Big Trees seems puny in comparison to their weight of up to 12 million pounds. The deepest roots are only 4 feet under the tree, and if the moisture supply to the soil is good, the lateral spread of the roots will measure only 40 to 50 feet out from the base of the tree.

Right: A young tree flanked by giants in a grove of Sierra redwoods.

Far right: The Giant Forest seen from Log Meadow during the late spring runoff from melted snow.

In soil that does not receive or hold adequate moisture, however, the lateral roots may grow out as far as 125 feet from the base, covering a total area of more than 1 acre.

Like their coastal relatives, the Sierra redwoods are named for the color of their bark, which is cinnamon red in a mature tree. The bark provides an impressive protective layer, for it measures up to 2 feet thick in some trees and is generally about 1 foot thick. This covering is spongy and deeply furrowed, often showing signs of repeated fires that it has stopped from reaching the living wood of the tree.

The wood that is so well protected in the giant sequoia is quite similar in appearance to that of the coast redwood; it is dark red and has approximately the same weight and texture as the coast variety. Yet for all its size, the Big Tree's wood does not possess the strength of its relative's; the Sierra redwood tends to shatter when it falls, its wood breaking across the grain into short, jagged segments. This lack of lateral strength is the reason giant sequoias are no longer cut for timber; when these trees were heavily logged in the latter half of the nineteenth century, at least half of every tree was wasted in the felling.

The foliage of Sierra redwoods, which resembles that of juniper or cypress trees, is composed of awl-shaped leaves that measure

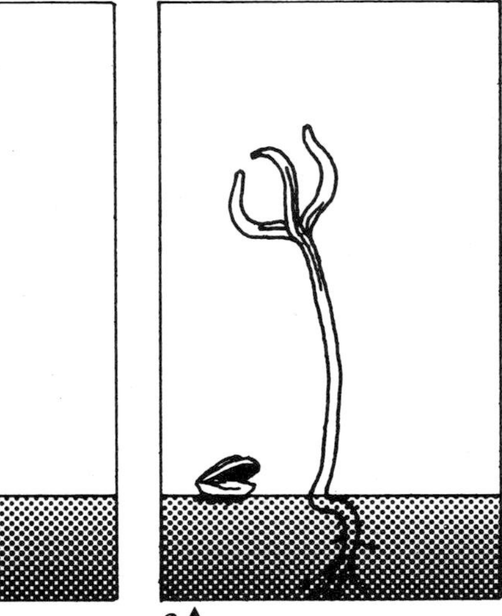

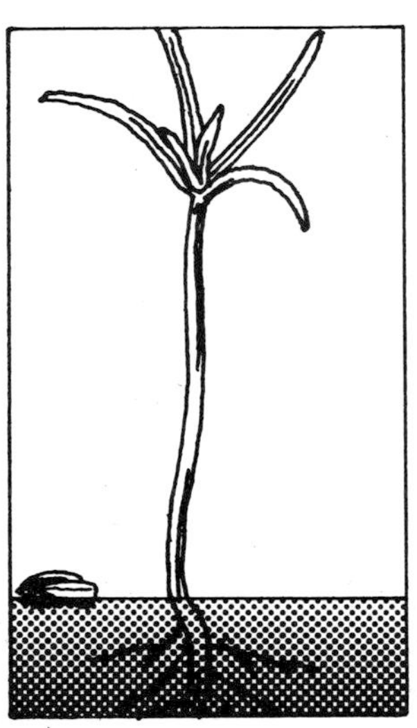

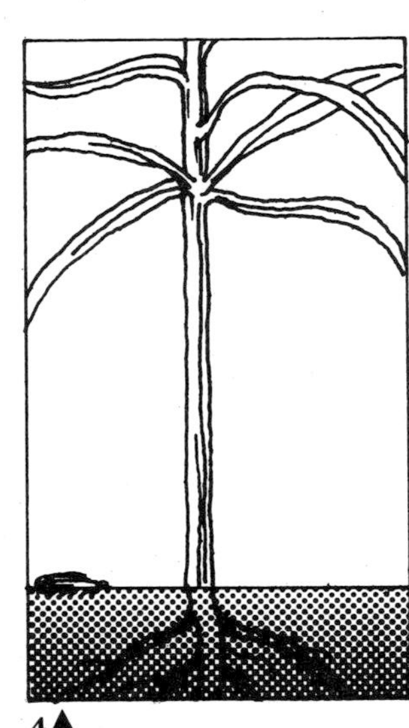

Right: The stages of development of a giant sequoia. (1) Germination with the seedling still in a shell. (2) After the shell has popped off. (3) After the cotyledons (embryonic leaves) have spread out. (4) With secondary leaves forming at center. These young seedlings are not very shade tolerant in their first few years.

Right: Foliage of the Sierra redwood, which resembles that of the juniper.

Below: Five of the tiny giant sequoia seeds on a penny.

only 1/12 to $\frac{1}{2}$ inch in length. The seed-bearing cones grow on the ends of branchlets; the cones are $1\frac{1}{2}$ to $2\frac{3}{4}$ inches long. Each cone contains 150 to 250 tiny seeds, which measure 91,000 to a pound. Although the giant sequoia also develops burls on its trunk, like its coastal relative, these burls do not contain eyes and thus cannot sprout under any conditions.

The principal sources of moisture for these trees' growth and germination are the rains and snows of spring and winter months, but the thunderstorms of summer also play an important role in the life and death of Sierra redwoods. Some moisture nourishes the trees from the frequent but brief summer rains, and all too often the lightning of these storms hit the tops of the large trees. Sometimes a lightning strike will ignite the dry crown of a tree and the resulting fire will spread across the tops of other trees, creating a forest fire that is too high for ground equipment to fight. Fortunately, a crown fire will not usually kill a giant sequoia, although fire or lightning victims can often be identified by their 'snag tops'—irregular growth of crown foliage and an exposed, jagged-looking section of upper trunk. Ground fires, also caused by lightning much of the time, are not likely to kill the giant trees, but they can do damage to the wood and roots that will eventually cause the tree to develop a snag top by inhibiting adequate moisture and food from reaching as far up as the tree's crown.

Fires have beneficial as well as damaging effects on the Sierra redwoods. Because ground fires burn the organic material on the forest floor and in the top layer of soil, they create the ideal—and necessary—conditions for germination of the giant sequoia's seeds. Although the tiny seeds, which fall from dry cones on the tree at a rate of about 300,000 per year, can occasionally germinate on open ground, they fare much better if they are buried lightly in the soil. When a fire consumes the fallen branchlets and small plants on the soil surface, it leaves tiny holes that the tree's seeds fall into, allowing a favorable percentage of them to germinate. In addition, fires interrupt the growth cycles of other plants in this forest, favoring the longevity and new growth of the Sierra redwood. This dependence on wildfire has led one expert in the ecology of sequoias to conclude that 'there is a high probability that, without fire, the giant sequoia would not today be an extant species.'

Below left: Uncontrolled fire burning in the crown of forest conifers. Such fires often are caused by lightning from the summer storms that are common to mountain terrain; before modern aerial firefighting techniques, nothing could be done to stop this high-altitude burning.

Below: The Grizzly Giant, a classic example of nature's urge for survival. This tree had its crown broken off by lightning and subsequent fire, and later fires caused further damage and mis-shaping that inspired the tree's name. Yet this indomitable giant lives on.

Preceding pages: A large grove of giant sequoias of varying sizes and ages, near Round Meadow in Sequoia National Park.

Right: The Bachelor and Three Graces in Mariposa Grove, Yosemite National Park, in an 1870 photo.

ALMOST AGELESS

UNTIL 1953, THE GIANT SEQUOIA, at up to 3500 years old, was thought to be the oldest living tree as well as the largest. Recent studies of the bristlecone pine, found in the arid White Mountains of eastern California, have shown one living specimen to be as old as 4600 years and several other trees to be more than 4000 years old. These ancient survivors do not look at all mammoth, though—they are stunted, gnarled growths about 25 feet high that cling to the earth in their harsh environment.

Another possible contender for the old-age title is a stand of Douglas firs in British Columbia, found in the 1960s, which scientists believe was buried by an Ice Age glacier about 40,000 years ago. When the glacier receded, the hypothesis goes, the affected trees resumed growth. However, further studies are needed to confirm this hypothesis.

In recent years, the estimated ages of Sierra redwoods have been revised downward. In 1894, John Muir, the most famous champion of the giant sequoias and the Sierra Nevada wilderness, made an unconfirmed notation that he had counted 4000 growth rings on a sequoia stump, but modern, more precise core samplings and careful ring counts show a maximum age of

Below and left: The Grizzly Giant. On the right is Galen Clark, who discovered the Mariposa Grove where this tree stands.

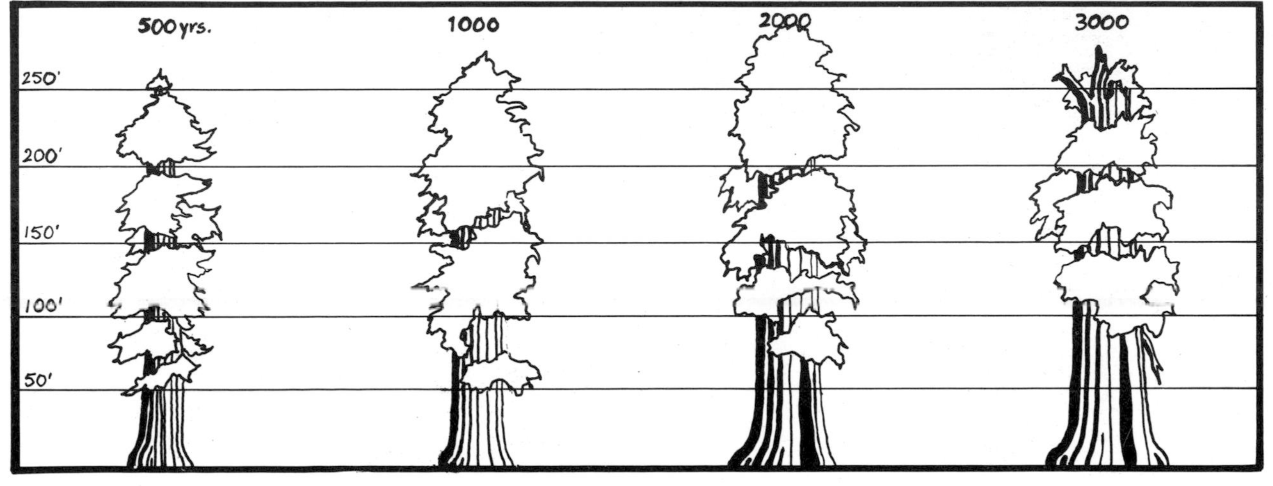

Left: Comparative height and age of a giant sequoia's growth; note that the crown diminishes and the trunk broadens after the tree reaches 2000 years of age.

3500 years for the giant sequoia. The General Sherman Tree, though largest of all, is less than 2500 years old. In fact, its mighty size and relative youth qualify the Sherman tree for another title—the fastest-growing on earth. The second-largest sequoia, the General Grant, is estimated to be 2000 years old, and the famous 'tunnel tree' in Yosemite National Park, named the Wawona Tree, was measured at approximately 2200 years old when it fell in 1969.

The Grizzy Giant of Mariposa Grove, now a part of Yosemite National Park, was long thought to be the oldest of all sequoias. Galen Clark, who discovered the Mariposa Grove and was the first government-appointed 'guardian' of the Yosemite grant which preceded its designation as a park, guessed that the Grizzly Giant could be no younger than 6000 years old. Subsequent estimates suggested a more modest 3800 years for this weathered and craggy tree. More accurate recent dating methods have again revised those guesses, placing an age limit of 2500 years on this aged-looking giant.

John Muir pointed out another factor that adds to the impact and longevity of these monumental trees. In 1878, in his description of the giant sequoia forests, he wrote that when the Grizzly Giant falls, its traces will remain clearly evident for at least another thousand years, even if the trunk and limbs and foliage of the tree were all to disappear immediately. The ditch that the tree's trunk would make and the hole left by its roots would be so immense that forest matter would not fill them, Muir wrote. Furthermore, even if new growth sprouted in the wake of this fallen giant, the pattern of this growth would still indicate the shape of no other thing but a sequoia.

Right: Another view of The Grizzly Giant, which has survived numerous fires and lightning strikes, and also suffers the effects of popularity. As much as an acre of the ground surrounding this tree is so severely packed down by visitors' feet that poor drainage of rainwater has eroded the soil and exposed some roots.

Below: Mule deer in the Sierra redwood habitat.

THE SEQUOIA COMMUNITY

EQUALLY IMPORTANT TO THE GIANT SEQUOIA'S continued growth and regeneration is its forest environment. One common inhabitant of the Sierra groves is the chickaree, or Douglas squirrel, which is the only animal that derives nourishment from the Big Tree. This rodent eats the seeds of many conifers in the giant sequoia's growth zone, but it prefers to dine on the green scales of the tree's cones, pulling them to pieces and peeling the flesh off the scales with its teeth. As the squirrel feeds, the tiny seeds that lodge under the cone scales are released, and since the animal usually feeds high up in the tree, it is the agent of scattering seeds across a wide area.

The chickaree also drops many cones from the tree before eating them; then it climbs to the ground and stores the cones for future food supplies. Often it buries the cones under the litter covering the forest floor, thereby increasing the chances for any seeds that separate from the cones to germinate in the moist soil and

1▲

2▲

3▲

4▼

5▼

6▲

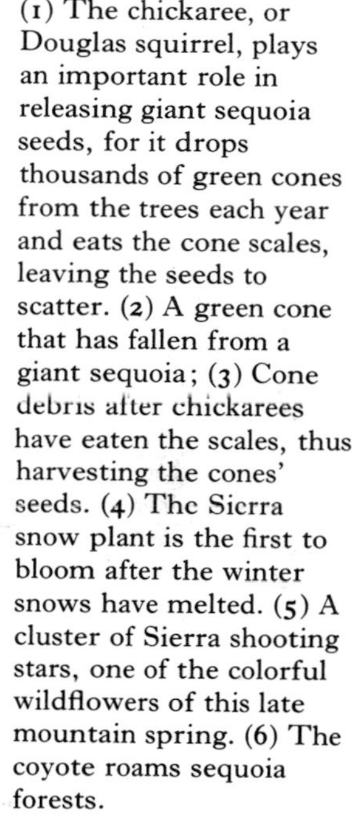

(1) The chickaree, or Douglas squirrel, plays an important role in releasing giant sequoia seeds, for it drops thousands of green cones from the trees each year and eats the cone scales, leaving the seeds to scatter. (2) A green cone that has fallen from a giant sequoia; (3) Cone debris after chickarees have eaten the scales, thus harvesting the cones' seeds. (4) The Sierra snow plant is the first to bloom after the winter snows have melted. (5) A cluster of Sierra shooting stars, one of the colorful wildflowers of this late mountain spring. (6) The coyote roams sequoia forests.

sprout up through the layers of fallen organic material. When the squirrel returns to feed on its buried treasure, it usually eats a quantity of cones in one place, leaving behind a pile of seeds that also have increased chances of sprouting because the top layers provide protection for the bottom ones.

A tiny beetle, $\frac{1}{8}$ inch long, likewise participates in the fragile process of regeneration for this giant tree. The long-horned wood-boring beetle deposits its eggs on the scales of the cones, and its larvae chew into the interior of the cone after they hatch. The destruction of the cone tissue causes the cone scales to turn brown and dry out, which in turn releases a flurry of seeds.

The other animals inhabiting a Sierra redwood community do not participate directly in the trees' growth cycle or benefit directly from it. Bird populations are a particularly striking feature of these groves. At least 30 avian species breed in or near the trees. The most numerous birds in old-growth and mixed sequoia forests are the mountain chickadee, Oregon junco, western robin, Steller's jay, western tanager and nuthatch. Several species of hawks and owls also live among the trees, finding food in open areas of the forest floor.

Larger animals are likewise populous in the Big Tree groves, but most are nocturnal and shy of people and thus are not easily seen. In addition to the chickaree, common mammals include the deer mouse, gray squirrel, mule deer, coyote and black bear. More rare inhabitants of this territory are the Trowbridge shrew, bobcat, marten, long-tailed weasel and the mountain lion. Several types of lizards and snakes are found in the Sierra redwood forests, including the western rattlesnake.

Opposite: Pacific dogwoods blooming against a background of red firs and ponderosa pines in the Giant Forest. The dogwood grows well in shade, providing a useful undercover in giant sequoia forests.

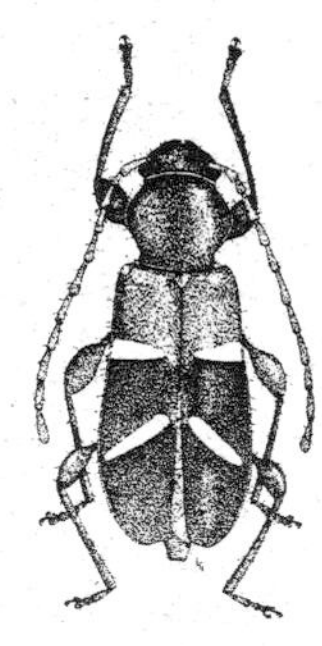

Above: The long-horned wood-boring beetle, *Phymatodes nitidus*, the beetle responsible for seed dispersal from the crowns of Big Trees. Its larvae eat the flesh of cones, slowly killing them and causing the seeds to fall from the dry, lifeless husks.

Right: Since the grizzly bear became extinct in California about 30 years ago, the black bear is now the largest mammal in Sierra forests.

Below: A drawing of the rarely seen marten, which preys on smaller animals of the sequoia community, including the chickaree.

The giant sequoia also shares its forest with numerous other plants. By their size and height, the mature sequoias dominate, but their more delicate seedlings must compete for light with such trees as the sugar pine, ponderosa pine, Douglas fir, incense cedar, western yew and species of oak and maple. Although the Sierra groves are less damp and undergo greater changes in temperature than groves of coast redwoods trees, several types of ferns also flourish with the giant sequoias. Among them are the bracken fern, wood fern, lady fern, sword fern and bird-foot fern.

The flowers and shrubs abundant among the Big Trees include larkspur, buttercup, mock orange, thimbleberry, wild strawberry, lupine, trillium and bush chinquapin. The list of ground cover varieties, bushes and flowers in this rich mountain environment numbers at least 120 specimens, most of which blossom in the early summer.

One recent study has uncovered evidence that increased human population of the giant sequoia groves—in the form of temporary visitors, but in great numbers—may have stimulated the activity of a potentially damaging pest among the trees. Carpenter ants, which find food in plant and animal debris, have recently increased in number in some groves, a development thought to be related to the greater availability of food scraps from visitors' picnics and campgrounds. Carpenter ants live in large colonies in the bark of giant sequoias, as well as in fallen trees or dead stumps. Although the colonies make ugly holes in the bark of living trees, the ants' impact is too small to affect the trees' growth. The ants' potential for harming the trees is related to the chambers the ants burrow for their young. These channels can go as deep as 20 feet into a tree, thereby creating pathways by which more dangerous organisms can penetrate the sequoia's bark and damage the wood itself.

Far right: The western porcupine, seldom seen by human visitors to Big Tree forests.

Below, from left to right: Trees of the Sierra zone: incense cedar in its prime; mature ponderosa pine; and mature sugar pine some 220 feet tall.

LARGEST LIVING THINGS

To date, the only real threats to these massive trees come from far greater disruptions than ant colonies or other small pests. Until the vast majority of giant sequoias were legally set aside, primarily from 1890 to the 1920s, logging was their most virulent killer. Now that they are protected from commercial exploitation, the only source of wholesale death for these long-lived giants would be some dramatic alteration in climate, such as a harsh, years-long drought or a sudden, severe cooling of their growing area.

The giant sequoia's invulnerability results from a combination of assets, but for the mature tree, size is clearly the dominating feature. The General Sherman Tree, the biggest tree of all, is located in Sequoia National Park. This tree was discovered in 1879 by a hunter, James Wolverton, who named it for the officer under whom he had served in the Civil War. As noted previously, the tree's dimensions are staggering: height, 272.4 feet; circumference at base, 101.6 feet; diameter at base, 34.3 feet; height of largest branch, 130 feet; and diameter of largest branch, 6.8 feet—the latter itself a respectable size for a tree. The estimated weight of this leviathan, 12 million pounds, includes 750,000 pounds of roots and 14,000 pounds of bark. If cut for timber, the General Sherman Tree would yield 600,120 board feet of lumber, which would not

Above: Mariposa Grove and the Guardian's Cabin in an early photograph. Galen Clark, who discovered this grove, lived here as the original steward of the Yosemite territory.

Left: The gnarled roots of Old Goliath, which stood in the South Calaveras Grove until 1861. Young seedlings of giant sequoia now flourish all around this fallen tree, and a dogwood has become established among the upturned roots.

GENERAL SHERMAN

only make 40 five-room houses but would result in a box that could hold an ocean liner.

A close second to this tree is the General Grant Tree, in King's Canyon National Park. Its vital statistics are a height of 267.4 feet, circumference of 107.6 feet, and a base diameter of 35.7 feet. Its overall volume is less than that of the General Sherman, comprising 516,456 board feet of lumber if it were cut. Next in this magnificent pecking order is the Boole Tree, in Sequoia National Forest, named for the forester who insisted that it be left standing when all the old-growth sequoias around it were cut for timber. Its height is 268.8 feet and its circumference at the base of 112 feet is greater than the Grant or Sherman. The Boole Tree tapers significantly, though; its estimated lumber volume of 479,688 board feet ranks this tree third overall.

A few other trees approach the massive dimensions of the giant sequoias, although none has been claimed to surpass the sheer mass of this species. Specimens of the kauri pine, or Big Tree of New Zealand, have been measured at 24 feet in diameter, which would result in about 200,000 board feet of lumber. One tule cypress tree near Oaxaca, Mexico, though only 160 feet tall, has a diameter of 40 feet at its base and 35 feet at a height of 5 feet above the ground. Again, its combined height and mass do not match the sequoia's, but its diameter surpasses that of the General Grant Tree. One oddity among trees, the banyan, generates new trunks from roots that extend downward from its branches, in effect creating an aggregation of hundreds of trunks. If this arrangement were considered as one collective trunk, it would far outstrip any other tree, for the diameter of an old banyan unit measures 100 feet or more.

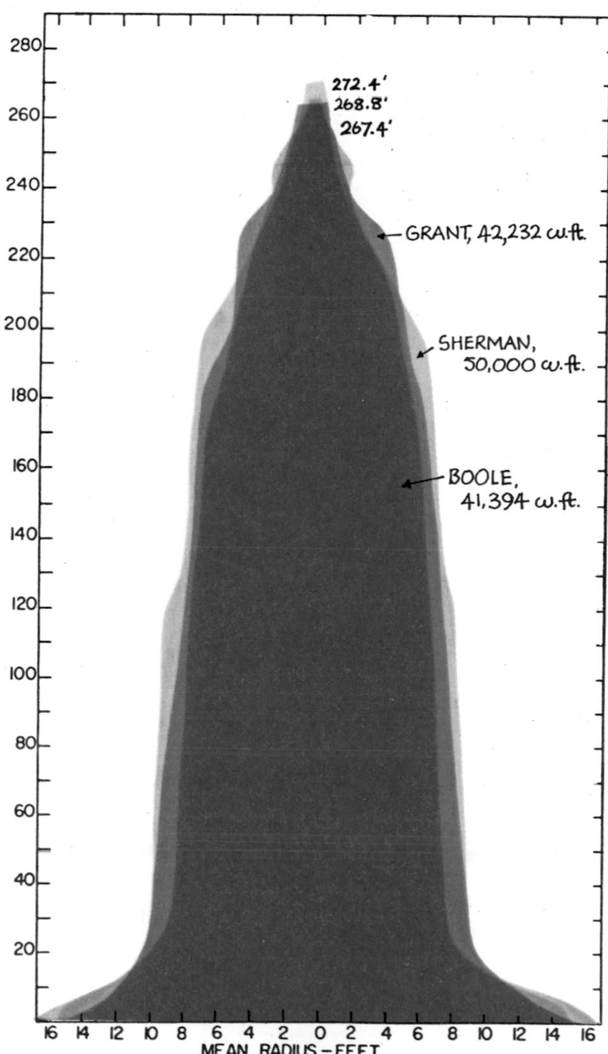

Opposite: The General Sherman Tree, in the Giant Forest of Sequoia National Park, is the world's largest tree by volume. Probably it is also the world's fastest-growing tree, with an annual production of 40 cubic feet of new wood—the equivalent of a tree that grows from a seedling to 50 feet in height and 1 foot in diameter in 1 year.

Above left: A fallen limb from a giant sequoia testifies to the immense size of these trees. This limb is as large as the trunk of many large trees.

Far left: The General Grant Tree, the world's second-largest tree, in a view showing the massive trunk, or bole. This tree is located in Kings Canyon National Park.

Left: The comparative volume of the largest giant sequoias, the General Sherman, General Grant and Boole Tree.

Following pages: The felling of the Mark Twain Tree in Kings Canyon National Park, 1891. This immense, unscarred specimen was cut down for exhibition; one section of the base may be seen at the American Museum of National History in New York. Sadly, the proud loggers downed what may have been the most perfect Big Tree of them all.

THE DAWN'S LEGACY

The coast redwood and giant sequoia are descendants of the first conifers, which were born in the Triassic period of geologic time, more than 200 million years ago. Conifers were the first true trees, and they dominated forests that virtually covered the earth during the dinosaurs' time. Throughout a slow succession of geologic changes, and a more rapid series of climatic ones, the species of sequoia have found their limits and their natural homes.

The periods of geologic time are so immense that even a tree that lives 20 or 30 centuries seems a miniscule achievement in comparison. Yet few living things have the geologic consistency and continuity that redwood trees demonstrate. Their first evidence, in the form of fossilized cones, dates from the Upper Jurassic period, some 130 million years ago. Pterodactyls, the ancient flying reptiles, and brontosaurs, the huge vegetarians, probably inhabited these first sequoia forests, and the earth's continents had not yet begun to thrust up their major mountain ranges.

Conifers met their 'modern' rivals in the next geologic period, the Cretaceous, when deciduous trees developed. During the 60 million years of this age, dinosaurs became extinct, plant life diversified into forests that resembled those of today, and the great seas that covered much of western North America, southern Europe and south Russia began to recede. What are now the frigid arctic regions were temperate expanses where the burgeoning forests could grow without barrier; the Aleutian land bridge joined Alaska and Siberia, thus linking the ancient trees of Asia and America.

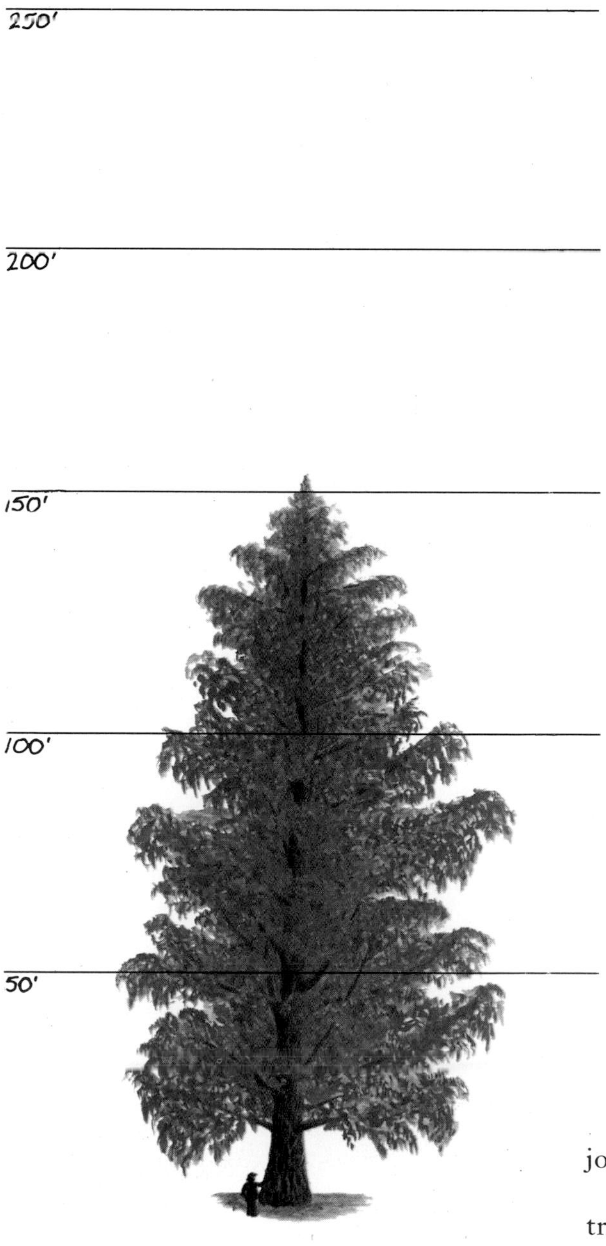

Opposite: A cultivated dawn redwood, planted in the San Francisco area about 30 years ago.

GLOBAL FORESTS

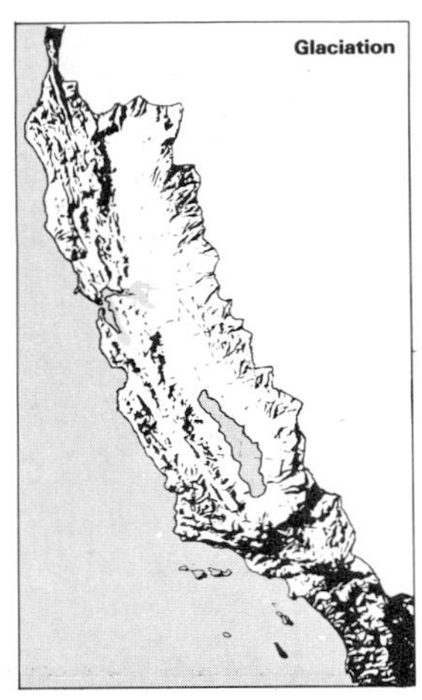

Above: The probable extent of glaciation during the Ice Age, from the Klamath and Cascade Ranges in the north along the Sierra Nevada ridge as far south as the eastern Transverse Ranges of California.

THE FORESTS FLOURISHED AND THEIR SPECIES became ever more sophisticated during the Cenozoic era, called the 'Age of Recent Life.' By geologic definition, recent life began some 70 million years ago, when trees were distributed over the greatest area of the globe and were most dominant, populating the then-warm lands of Greenland, Alaska and Spitzbergen, as well as lower temperate areas that still support such forest life.

The redwoods were in the thick of the tree population during this time. Twelve or more species of sequoia and metasequoia fossils have been identified, dating from the Cretaceous period onward. One species, *Sequoia langsdorfi,* closely resembled the coast redwood, and another, *Sequoia reichenbachi*, left fossil cones much like those of the giant sequoia. Another common fossil of the sequoia group had foliage similar to that of *Sequoia sempervirens* but showed a different arrangement of cones and branchlets; this specimen was assigned a separate generic name, *Metasequoia,* because of its botanical distinctions.

The redwood forebears of the coastal and Sierra trees, as well as the *Metasequoia,* thrived in forests from Alaska and Canada to France, England, Germany and across Asia to China and Japan. In the United States, fossil remains have been found in Pennsylvania, Kansas, Texas, Colorado, Nevada, Wyoming, Idaho and the Pacific Coast states. Another species, *Sequoia ambigua,* was found in Mexico. As the planet's climate grew ever cooler, beginning about a million years ago, all the northern forests retreated southward, until the four great global ice flows drove them to their present ranges or wiped them out altogether.

Before the Ice Age, the closest ancestors of the giant sequoia lived in Idaho and Nevada at least 10 million years ago, and possibly as much as 20 million years ago. These forests were cut off from the Pacific Ocean's life-giving supply of moisture when the Sierra Nevada mountains reached their full height and expanse. The sequoia migrated westward through some open passes in this new barrier of granite, and as the climate of the trees' original home became increasingly dry, these early sequoias became extinct everywhere east of the Sierra peaks.

Sequoia sempervirens likewise reached beyond its present limits at one time. Fossils of this tree's progenitors have been found beneath lava deposits at the base of Mt. Shasta, which is

Right: A petrified fallen giant. This specimen, 68 feet long and 11 feet in diameter, reclines in the Petrified Forest of Sonoma County, where 300 trees cover some 20 acres. All were turned to stone by the heat and blast of a nearby volcano.

now part of a hot, dry valley nearly a hundred miles east of the coast. Graphic fossil evidence of this species exists as far inland as Colorado's Florissant Petrified Forest and the Specimen Ridge Petrified Forest in Yellowstone National Park.

The most extensive grouping of ancient redwoods is preserved closer to the living trees' present range, however. Near Calistoga, California, about 70 miles north of San Francisco, is a collection of 300 stone trees covering 20 acres that were buried in a volcanic eruption some 5 million years ago. The private park where the remains of this redwood forest can be inspected is a few miles from a California volcano named Mount St Helena (not to be confused with the recently active Mount St Helens in Washington). The force of the volcano's explosion and lava flow toppled the forests around it; all the petrified trees are pointing away from the mountain.

This petrified logjam was discovered in 1871 by a homesteader, Charlie Evans, who was clearing the property for a pasture. Evans realized that his fallen forest would be more valuable than the unfinished pasture, so he uncovered the logs, whose bark, though petrified, was intact and even showed axe marks in some places. Evans hung out a sign announcing 'The Petrified Forest' and charged 50 cents admission to visitors, who could inspect an 80-foot trunk, the 'Queen of the Forest,' which lay in segments, as well as a fallen 'Monarch,' a 125-foot redwood with a diameter of 8 feet and growth rings revealing its age to be at least 1000 years. The intense heat of the eruption had consumed most of the trees' roots, foliage and upper branches, but some remnants of cones and leaves also remain in this fossil graveyard.

Left: A sequoia fossil trunk in Yellowstone National Park, where both *Metasequoia* and early forms of *Sequoia* trees once grew.

Left: The world distribution of all three types of redwood trees; this map shows both present growing areas and fossil sites.

Below: The pteranodon (a flying reptile) and an ichthyosaurus, two of the animals that probably coexisted with the early redwoods in California in the late Cretaceous period.

DAWN REDWOOD: A LIVING FOSSIL

One of the original members of the redwood family that grew throughout the earth's forests in the distant geologic past was *Metasequoia glyptostroboides,* now called the dawn redwood. This tree, which is deciduous, grew in western North America along with the ancestors of coast and Sierra redwoods, and it was the species that spread across the northern section of the temperate zone in what are now arctic regions. Because no metasequoia fossils were found to be less than 20 million years old, this species was believed to be extinct until the 1940s.

In 1944, a Chinese forester named T Wang discovered a large tree in the province of Szechuan, in central China, that he could not identify. He collected specimens of this tree and took them to a university professor, Dr. W C Cheng, who realized that this species was unlike anything known to have lived in China. Cheng consulted another scientist, H H Hu, who determined the specimens to be identical with fossils of metasequoia found in Japan and Manchuria. These botanists shared a truly rare event in science—the discovery of a living species believed to have become extinct millions of years before.

The Chinese scientists published their findings in a technical journal in their country and sent specimens of the newly discovered tree to two American experts. One of these men, paleontologist Ralph W Chaney of the University of California, found that the specimens bore a remarkable resemblance to metasequoia fossils that he had unearthed near the John Day River in Oregon. Chaney was determined to see the living tree himself, and in 1948 he and science editor Milton Silverman of the San Francisco *Chronicle* departed for China.

Their trip was nothing like a visit to one of California's redwood parks: the men flew to Chunking, took a river boat down the Yangtze to a town called Wan-hsien, and then walked over mountainous and mud-slippery terrain for three days to reach the interior of Szechuan, where Wang had found the reported dawn redwood. Because local residents warned that bandits were in the area, the visitors were escorted on the last leg of their journey by a motley crew of soldiers carrying antiquated rifles.

When they reached the valley of Mo-tao-chi, where the tree had been found, these first white men ever to visit this remote part of China immediately became the center of attention. On their excursion to the bank of a rice paddy to see

Right: Three young dawn redwoods (*Metasequoia glyptostroboides*) in central China, in their leafless winter condition.

Far right: Dr Ralph W Chaney and a Chinese official at the base of a mature dawn redwood in Szechuan Province, China. Paleontologist Chaney traveled to China in 1948 to document the discovery of these living trees by a Chinese forester in 1944.

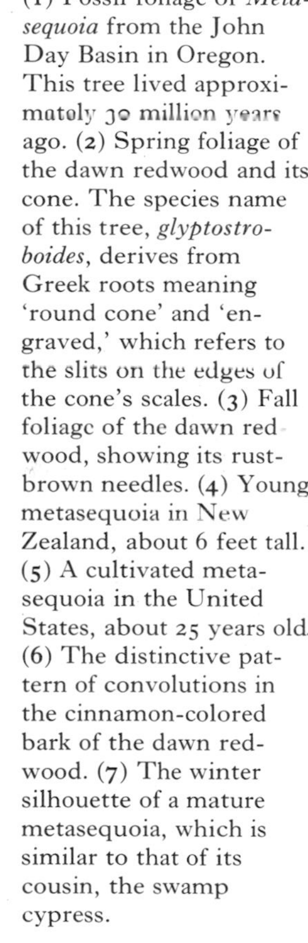

(1) Fossil foliage of *Metasequoia* from the John Day Basin in Oregon. This tree lived approximately 30 million years ago. (2) Spring foliage of the dawn redwood and its cone. The species name of this tree, *glyptostroboides*, derives from Greek roots meaning 'round cone' and 'engraved,' which refers to the slits on the edges of the cone's scales. (3) Fall foliage of the dawn redwood, showing its rust-brown needles. (4) Young metasequoia in New Zealand, about 6 feet tall. (5) A cultivated metasequoia in the United States, about 25 years old. (6) The distinctive pattern of convolutions in the cinnamon-colored bark of the dawn redwood. (7) The winter silhouette of a mature metasequoia, which is similar to that of its cousin, the swamp cypress.

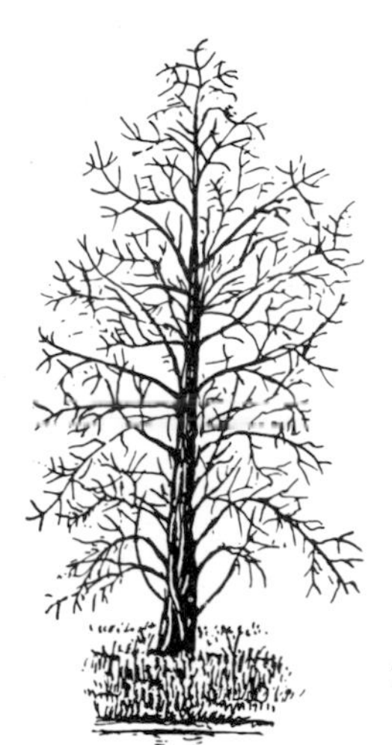
7

the tree, and two others nearby, they were accompanied by the entire population of the valley, including pigs and chickens. Still, Chaney confirmed his belief that the fossil and living trees were directly related, and the local Chinese told them that many more such trees grew in a more remote area in the neighboring province of Hupeh.

Chaney, Silverman and their guides and porters set out for the village of Shui-hsa-pa, where, Silverman wrote, 'we found a lost world —a world that existed more than a million years ago.' In the forests of this remote region, the American visitors counted more than a hundred of the dawn redwoods and estimated that hundreds more filled the neighboring valley, which is at approximately the same latitude as New Orleans and at an elevation of 4000 feet. According to incomplete local records, rainfall there is about 50 inches per year. The Hupeh trees did not rival either species of California sequoia in size—the largest metasequoia measured 60 to 90 feet in height.

The size of these redwood trees was of far less importance to Chaney than their existence and their forest neighbors. He noted that the natural mixture of ancient species in this mountain-ringed valley did not exist anywhere in the modern world, commenting that he had come upon 'a botanical alumni reunion.' This forest contained oak, sassafras, sweet gum and katsura trees, which had been associated only in fossil remnants until Chaney found them in the remote Chinese interior.

This small expedition gathered some seedlings and additional specimens of the thriving metasequoia trees, and then set out for Nanking. On the return trek, their escort was called into

Right: A mature dawn redwood at Mo-tao-chi in central China. The building at its base is a temple, for this tree has been a source of worship in Chinese culture.

action, killing one bandit and scaring off two others along the narrow trail. Before leaving for the United States, Chaney met with government officials to urge them to designate the dawn redwoods' habitat a protected area, although he received no promises of such action.

In 1965, however, Chinese officials established a preserve of the ancient trees, and forestry experts have propagated metasequoia widely in other parts of China as well. A team of American scientists who visited China in 1975 reported that metasequoia is one of the prime trees used in urban plantings, and another report notes that the dawn redwood has been propagated as a timber crop in several areas of central and southeastern China.

Comparative studies of the utility of metasequoia wood have determined that it is not suitable for commercial development by American timber standards, but some products are manufactured from this tree's lumber in China. Other wood products exported from China are made from a variety of Scots pine *(Pinus sylvestris)*, which is commonly called 'European redwood' and is marketed as redwood even though it is not related to sequoia or metasequoia. The majority of Chinese 'redwood' products probably are actually made of this red-colored pine, for this conifer is far more abundant in the forests of China than is metasequoia or the introduced coast redwood.

Chaney returned to the United States with four seedlings of the dawn redwood; he planted and carefully cultivated them on the campus of the University of California at Berkeley. Since this tree's reintroduction in 1949, it has been planted in a variety of locations beyond California; at least one young specimen currently thrives in the rather extreme winter-and-summer climate of Cleveland, Ohio. Nor can the Americans claim the only propagation program of metasequoia; thousands of seeds and seedlings have been distributed by the Save-the-Redwoods League and the Arnold Arboretum of Harvard University, and these fast-growing trees are now planted as decorative foliage throughout England, Europe and Asia.

During winter the dawn redwood is easily distinguished from its redwood relatives, for the tree loses its needlelike leaves then and reveals upward-pointing limbs near the top. Close examination yields other differences, such as the arrangement of leaves and branchlets in opposite pairs, rather than in spirals or alternate arrays as in the other sequoias. The dimensions of the dawn redwood also distinguish it from the California species; metasequoias grow to heights of 140 feet and measure only 6 feet in diameter at most, which is less than half the size of coast and Sierra redwoods. Still, the dawn redwood has won a rare battle with extinction, and—like its North American relatives—this graceful tree has earned the admiration and the protection of those who share its home.

Left: A dawn redwood that flourishes in Laurelhurst Park, Portland, Oregon. One forester working with these trees found that cuttings grow rapidly and easily in the favorable Oregon climate.

Far left: Son of Hu, headman of Shui-hsa-pa village, Hupeh, photographed in front of a mature dawn redwood by Dr Ralph Chaney.

NATIVE AMERICAN WILDERNESS

Archaeological evidence shows that human inhabitants lived along the California coast as long ago as 2000 BC—coincidentally, at the time the oldest living coast redwoods were seedlings. These primitive peoples represented a culture known as the Middle Horizon, which later evolved into the Late Horizon culture. Both were marked by elementary tool making, and the later group developed the pointed arrow, more organized methods of gathering acorns and seeds, and large mortars for grinding the food. Although the early populations of the Sierra Nevada are less well documented than the coastal groups, similar peoples are believed to have lived in the foothills and valleys of these mountains. In both of the sequoia ranges, these primitive people continued to develop, forming the basis for the varied tribes of Indians who lived among the redwoods.

Some 200,000 Indians were living in California when the first white explorers pushed into the region. The early residents of the coast and Sierra redwoods' domain were among the 117 California tribes that have been documented, and each of these peoples developed a culture and language of its own. For those who came into contact with the redwoods, the colossal trees became a part of their lives, often as symbols of their spiritual beliefs and practices.

In the Sierra Nevada mountains, the Mono tribe believed the giant sequoia trees to be sacred, not to be harmed or utilized. These Indians thought that the spirit of the owl protected the huge trees, and their name for the sequoia derived from the Monos' imitation of the owl's call—*woh-woh-nau,*

Opposite: A grove of giant sequoias in the fog of late winter, as Indians and settlers would have seen them generations ago.

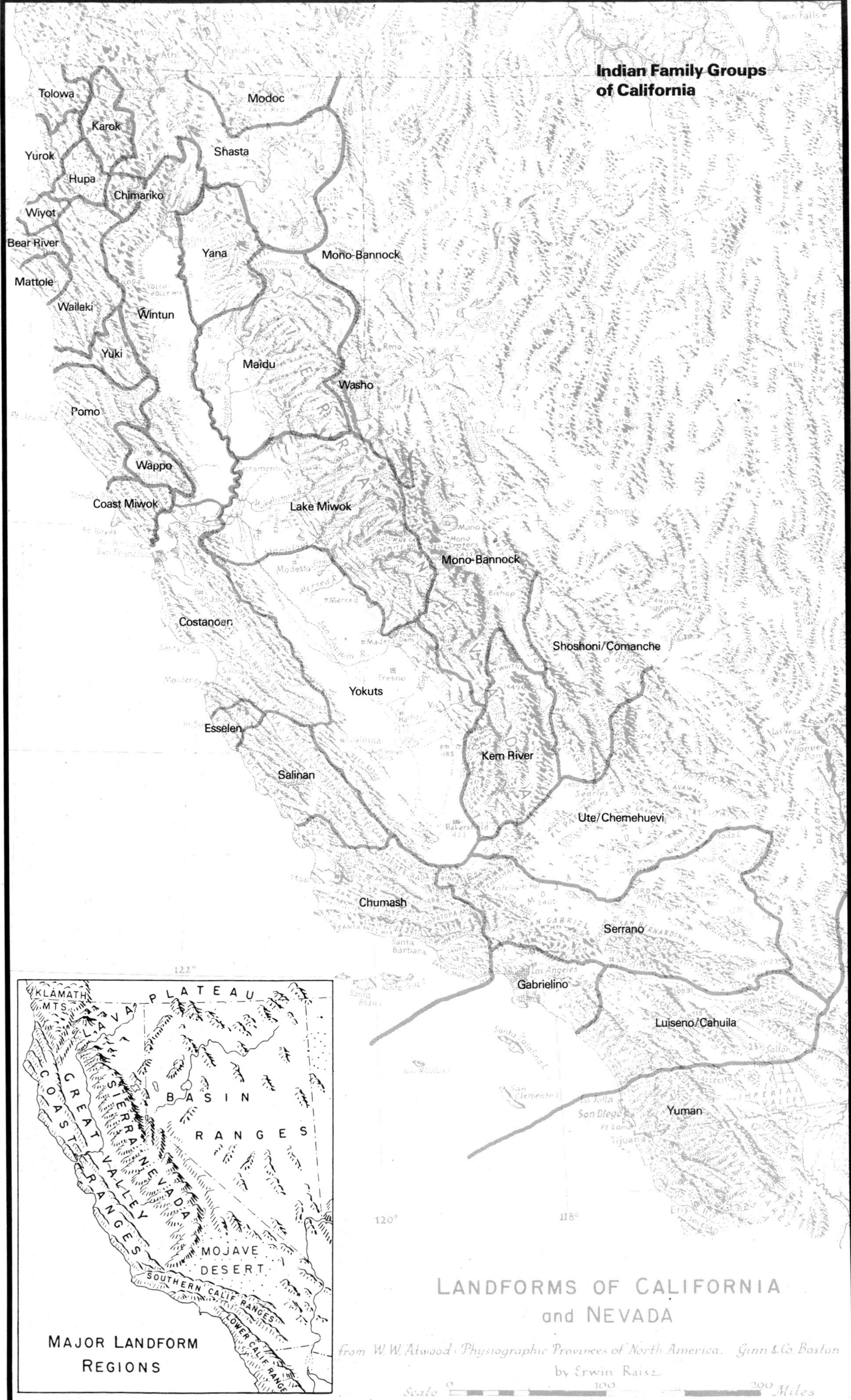

Right: Map of California showing Indian tribal family groupings in the mid-1800s.

or *wawona,* the name given to the famous tree through which a tunnel was cut after the Mariposa Grove of Yosemite was settled by white men. Another mountain tribe, the Miwok, had taboos against disturbing the giant sequoias, and used only the bark of fallen trees to build their primitive houses.

Along the Pacific Coast, the Indians made use of redwoods in their lifestyle and commerce. At least a dozen tribes occupied the forest lands along the coastal rivers and inland from the ocean; their villages were isolated by the natural boundaries of canyons, cliffs and dense forests, and neighboring tribes had little contact with one another. In the immediate vicinity of their villages, however, the Indians knew the terrain intimately, and this knowledge ensured both their sustenance and their protection.

The Yurok tribe, which lived near the mouth of the Klamath River in northern California, made extensive use of the coast redwoods. These Indians built crude but lasting homes of redwood planks, which they split from fallen or driftwood logs using elk-horn wedges and primitive adzes made from mussel shells. The boards used in Yurok houses were several inches thick and 1 to 4 feet wide, forming a structure about 20 feet square. The Indians made the walls of a dwelling by setting two rows of planks into the ground, one inside the other, and they formed the several-tiered roof by laying a

Left: A Tolowa Indian woman of Del Norte County on the northern California coast. She is wearing traditional tribal dress, in a scene from about 1890.

Below: A Wailuki Indian village on Ten Mile River in Mendocino County, in northern California. The Indians' dwellings, called wickiups, were built with discarded redwood planks from the coastal lumber mills. The coastal tribes were harassed and murdered by white settlers in this region, and the warfare prompted the US government to build forts in the 1850s. Ulysses S Grant served at the Eureka fort in 1853 and 1854.

double layer of planks on top of ridge poles and the side walls. The durability of both the Yuroks' construction methods and the redwood planks is demonstrated by the survival of several of these houses for more than a hundred years.

The Yuroks' favorable location near the mouth of a large river also provided them with a source of commerce. They built dugout canoes from the redwood logs that littered the nearby beaches, first burning the logs into canoe-length sections, then, using simple tools, splitting the logs and smoothing off the two surfaces. To hollow out the center of the log, they spread pitch over the area desired and set fire to the pitch, controlling the size and depth of the burn by smothering its flames with green bark. When the rough shape had been given to the boat, the Yurok craftsmen again smoothed its surfaces with their tools and finally polished it with stones.

Construction of such a canoe would take two Indians several months, and the final product would bring a high price from neighboring tribes upriver. The average boat, about 18 feet long, could navigate the river rapids and the shoreline ocean waves, and a few larger canoes, up to 42 feet long, were built to carry several-ton loads of fish from ocean waters. When the early white settlers built towns along the coast, they purchased canoes from the

Right: Yurok Indian dwelling in Humboldt County. The vertical redwood boards are 'planted' in the ground to form strong walls that frame the building. These Indians originally used redwood bark from fallen trees for their dwellings.

Right: Yosemite Indian woman in front of a wickiup in a photo from the 1880s. These miwok Indians of the Sierra region used much giant sequoia bark for their shelter.

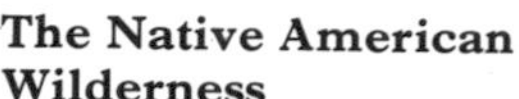

Yuroks for $10.00 to $30.00 each.

Other coast Indian tribes used the bark of fallen redwood trees for dwellings and smaller objects. The Sinkyone and Pomo people built small houses of bark; these structures were no longer than 15 feet across, and their roofs were lower than 6 feet. Pomo women made skirts of shredded bark from redwoods, and members of this tribe and others wove baskets from root fibers.

Although the Indians' use of redwood trees was largely limited to the abundant supply of fallen wood, some of the very first forest dwellers did fell trees when none were already available. They accomplished this with no metal tools, instead using heated stones to burn away part of the tree and continually scraping off the charred wood. When a hole had been burned on one side, these primitive loggers burned a similar place on the other side of the tree, but higher up on the trunk. While one group of Indians would make the second burn, another group would prepare the ground where the tree was to fall, making a 'bed' of logs and branches to hold the huge tree's weight. When they had felled the tree, the loggers would use

Left: Pomo Indians of the northern California coast, shown here pounding acorns for food. These Indians are well known for their baskets and weaving, for which they often used fibers from the pliable coast redwood bark.

Left: A Yurok Indian canoe. The basic early coastal California vessel was hollowed out of a split log by Indian craftsmen. These boats were so famous that other tribes traveled long distances to barter for them.

their wedges and heated stones to cut it into sections and planks. Of the 400 dwellings in the Klamath River area, however, only a few were made from redwoods that Indians cut down.

The towering redwoods also played a role in the spiritual life of coastal Indian tribes, as one surviving state landmark tree attests. During a time of drought, one tribe was forced from its upriver home to the Mad River delta along the Pacific, which was the home and hunting grounds for another tribe. The two tribes began warring over the territory, until, as legend has it, the Great Spirit communicated to them that rain would fall in the first tribe's home country if the chiefs of these two rivals would sit beside a certain redwood tree and conduct a peace ceremony. The chiefs did establish peace, and this tree became a place of special honor to the Indians. To mark the site of their peacemaking, the men of both tribes would shoot an arrow into the trunk of the tree each time they passed it, and the women would push a small green branch into the furrows of the tree's bark. After several generations of such tributes, the tree was covered with arrows and small branches, but in the 1880s a fire consumed almost all the tree and its decorative symbols. Indian Arrow Tree, as it is known, still stands, although it is a burned snag that no longer holds the offerings of its thankful neighbors.

Far right: A Shoshone-type tepee near the giant sequoias and white firs of what is now Sequoia National Park, in an engraving from the early 1800s.

Below: Yurok Indians wearing formal dress for their 'jump dance.' Their headdresses are made of woodpecker feathers; this bird of the coastal California forests had special significance to the Yuroks, as did their necklaces of dentalium shells, which were a form of money.

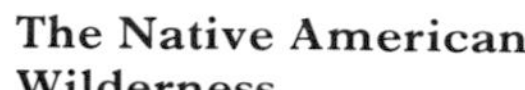

Left: Indians gathering food and firewood in the Sierra redwood region, probably members of the Mono/Bannock family, which spent summers in the mountains. Note the rifle in one man's hand in this 1877 view.

Below: Indians of Yosemite Valley in the early 1900s. These Indians have adopted white settlers' clothing for their work in the parklands of the area. Note the layers of Sierra redwood shakes on the roof of the dwelling in the background.

SETTLERS

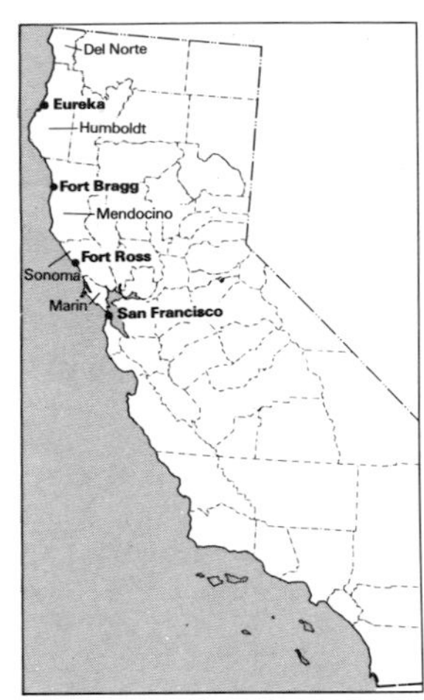

Above: Map of California showing the Russian settlements of Fort Ross and the Farallon Islands; also shown are the sites of Fort Bragg, Eureka and San Francisco.

Below and right: Two views of the chapel at Fort Ross before it was burned and subsequently rebuilt in the 1960's. This Russian-made redwood fort is now a state historic site; some of its original timbers are still intact.

Opposite: Redwoods near the Russian River, which meets the Pacific near Fort Ross.

THE FIRST PERMANENT SETTLEMENT established by newcomers to the coast redwoods region was Fort Ross, built by the Russians in 1812. These explorers purchased several hundred acres of forest and coastline property from the Indians residing there; the price was three blankets, two axes, three hoes and some beads and clothing. Like all sequoia forests in these tranquil years before logging and settling began in earnest, the Fort Ross site contained many fallen trees, and huge driftwood logs were to be found on the beaches below the coastal hills. The Russian builders made great use of this timber, and they cut some trees to make lumber and to clear growing areas.

Most of the lumber the Russians fashioned was used to construct a fort, whose surrounding walls measured 250 by 300 feet in length. The timbers in this barrier stood 15 feet above ground, and each log was set 3 feet into the ground. Blockhouses were built at two corners of the fort and three log houses were added inside the walls, providing a total of 22 rooms for the inhabitants. Several warehouses, a barracks for the garrisoned soldiers and a chapel were also built at Fort Ross—all of redwood.

The Russian settlers farmed some of their cleared fields, but the growing conditions were not suitable for the crops these farmers were accustomed to planting. Therefore, they turned to the sea as a major source of food and commodities to sell. They built several large ships, two of which were made primarily of redwood lumber, for sale to the Spanish or for use in their hunting of sea otters. The settlers were inexperienced in using their newly found timber, however, and they did not season the wood adequately before using it in the ships. The first of these craft, launched in 1822, was unfit for sailing five years later; the second ship, which weighed 2000 tons, proved unseaworthy after six years.

The ships and redwood logs figured in the Russians' settlements in one other way as well. The soldiers of Fort Ross carried supplies of firewood to their countrymen who had established an outpost on the Farallon Islands, about 30 miles west of San Francisco Bay. These low, rocky islands had no trees or other sources of adequate firewood, so redwood leftovers from Fort Ross were ferried to the inhabitants there. Although the transportation of redwood fuel was not a source of commerce for these first Russians, subsequent sailors did a thriving

Freeman Art Co.

business in this firewood in the late nineteenth century. The Russians' own experiment in colonizing this region ended in 1841, when they sold the fort and its site to John Sutter, whose name was to become synonymous with gold a few years later.

The Spanish had a less direct impact on the coast redwood forests, because they built mostly with adobe. Some of the beams in the larger structures they made were of redwood, though, and they marked some early exploration sites with simple crosses or boards of redwood. The founder of the Spanish missions in California, Fray Junipero Serra, must have recognized the lasting qualities as well as the beauty of the *Sequoia sempervirens,* for as he lay dying in 1784, the padre asked that his coffin be built of redwood. His request was granted and he was buried at Mission San Carlos Borromeo in Carmel. Although the church fell to ruins in later years, Fray Serra's coffin was discovered there 98 years later, completely intact.

Below: An 1853 engraving of a Gold Rush scene, from the Wells Fargo History Collection. The narrow, treacherous passes over the Sierra Nevada mountains to the western foothills were jammed with wagons and animals carrying prospectors and their goods.

The Gold Rush in the Sierra Nevada foothills brought great numbers of settlers and miners to both regions of California redwoods. Instead of the trickle of exploring parties across the mountains and through the groves of Big Trees that had come before, streams of Forty-niners poured through the mountain passes in search of quick fortunes. Smaller numbers of miners and entrepreneurs arrived by ship on their way to the Gold Country, and many more settlers sailed around Cape Horn to found cities on the Pacific Coast. San Francisco was instrumental in the trade and traffic to the gold fields, and all this new population claimed vast quantities of the coastal region's redwood forests for buildings, sidewalks and practically everything else.

Some businessmen did not limit their vision to conventional travel across the continent. When the United States acquired the California territory in 1848, at the end of the Mexican War, mail and supply routes and military protection suddenly were extended from coast to coast, though the transcontinental railroad was still a dream. One scheme promoted by some army officers and supported by such United States congressmen as Jefferson Davis (before the Civil War) was the importation of camels to transport supplies across the southwestern states to California. The experiment was approved and funded by Congress, and two boatloads of Egyptian camels arrived in Texas in 1856 and 1857.

Each of the animals carried loads of up to 1000 pounds and could travel as far as Los Angeles, but camels proved to be no more economical than mules or horses, and few handlers and drivers could be found to work with them. So the army decided to sell the camels, and the animals were driven to Benecia (northeast of San Francisco), the original capital of the state, for public auction. The animals were sold to one man, who subsequently dispersed them to ranches and homes in the Sacramento Valley and the hot, dry areas of Nevada.

Still believing in the possibilities of camel transport over the mountains, one San Francisco businessman, Otto Esche, imported a string of Bactrian camels from China, because these animals were native to a region similar to the Sierra Nevada. Esche planned to establish a regular pack train from San Francisco to Salt Lake City with the camels, but the venture never got under way. Esche sold the camels to another San Franciscan, who drove the nine survivors across the mountains for work in the Nevada mines in 1861. The route of this odd-looking expedition included the giant sequoia groves at Calaveras, where an artist who accompanied the pack train made a number of sketches of the improbable scene. The artist, Edward Vischer, published these drawings in his *Pictorial of California,* which features many views of the Sierra redwoods, with and without camels.

Many of the new Californians did not go to the mountains, but founded businesses to serve the miners and their boomtowns. One emigrant whose name is now a household word—Levi Strauss—arrived in San Francisco in 1853, planning to sell the canvas from his family's dry goods business as tents for the miners and loggers. He quickly determined that what these workmen needed more was a supply of sturdy clothing, and he fashioned britches from the heavy cloth he had brought with him. These work pants became popular immediately, and in 1860 Strauss added a new type of cloth to his clothing; he 'invented' demin when he ordered a strong cotton cloth from a manufacturer in Nimes, France. The cloth became known as 'de Nimes' and Levi's bluejeans were born when Strauss had all the cloth dyed with indigo to maintain a uniform color.

After the 1848 gold discovery at Coloma,

which sparked the rush of Forty-niners, another lode of gold was discovered at the headwaters of the Trinity River, farther north and west of the famous Sutter's Mill. This new mining territory was more easily reached by boat upstream from the mouth of the Trinity than by any overland route. Thus, thousands of prospective miners and settlers sailed to Humboldt Bay and became the first inhabitants of Eureka, from which they could travel upriver through the redwoods to the mines.

The impact of this great influx of people into California can be seen in the population figures

Left: Early miners in the Sierra Nevada foothills, wearing denim-type overalls in this view from the 1860s.

Above: The 1846 flag of the California republic.

Below: A scene by Edward Vischer showing the train of camels in the Calaveras Big Trees in 1861.

for the time: the state's population quadrupled during the decade from 1850 to 1860; within five years after gold was discovered, 150,000 people had passed through the formerly sleepy town of San Francisco; and Eureka, founded in 1850, had a population of 3000 by 1853.

The redwood forests felt the pressure of growth perhaps more dramatically than any other natural resource. At Eureka, where the virgin trees grew in huge groves all along the coastal hillsides and streambeds, the first sawmill was in operation within five months after the original boatload of settlers arrived. By the time this town had acquired 3000 residents, nine sawmills were slicing the redwoods into lumber, and in that year (1853) at least a hundred ships left Humboldt Bay with cargoes of redwood lumber totalling 20 million board feet. Within ten years of Eureka's founding, 300 sawmills were operating along the northern coast, and by 1870 the hills around Humboldt Bay were denuded of their magnificent sequoias.

One of the early sawmills south of Eureka was built by Harry Meiggs, a San Francisco alderman and importer. In 1851 he received a message that one of his ships bringing silk from the Orient had run aground up the coast, and Meiggs sent a crew to find the ship and salvage its cargo. The salvagers failed to find the wreck but instead discovered the untouched redwood forests along the Mendocino coast, and the entrepreneur decided to use his cargo ships for the valuable lumber from then on.

Meiggs knew that he had stumbled on a fortune, for he had participated in the logging of the San Antonio forest east of San Francisco Bay (the site of Berkeley and Oakland), and was aware that the demand for this durable

H Meiggs

Opposite: The barkentine *Jane L Stanford* with a cargo of redwood lumber from Eureka, bound for San Francisco Bay.

Right: Speculator Harry Meiggs, who gained and lost several fortunes during his notorious career, profited greatly from cutting and shipping Mendocino County redwoods to San Francisco and beyond.

Below: An 1860s photograph of a crew sawing the huge trunk of a coast redwood tree into sections as part of the mammoth logging operation at Little River in Mendocino County.

The woodsman's Cabin Humboldt C. Cal
Freeman Art C. Foto.

lumber was bringing $500.00 per 1000 board feet. Meiggs also had a ready supply of loggers, men who had cut the forests of the East Coast and had come to California to try their luck at mining, without success. The sawmill at Big River (now Mendocino, but briefly called Meiggstown) became a regular stop for ships carrying timber to San Francisco, Seattle and beyond. Meiggs himself was less fortunate than the loggers and shippers of the northern California coast, however; he got into financial trouble with other ventures and fled to South America.

Speculators such as Meiggs also had some laws to help them. The Preemption Law of 1841 and later the Homestead Act of 1862 encouraged settlement of the unpopulated lands, and many settlers took advantage of the opportunity provided by these laws to buy 160 acres of virgin timber for $1.25 per acre, the same price they would have paid for land on the plains or deserts. Some homesteaders did try to make farms of their wooded lands (many of which had already been cut over by fast-moving loggers); these persistent settlers had to keep the coast redwoods in check, which was difficult because of the trees' size and their ability to regenerate from stumps or fallen logs.

Less well-intended residents of the area used the homestead laws to defraud the government by hiring sailors and new immigrants who needed a fast dollar to file claims for legal homesteads in the heavily timbered lands. The law required that a settler live on the property for a year and build a dwelling there, but the claimants were seldom asked to prove that they were actual residents. Often agents would buy the title to a fraudulent homesteader's land, then sell it to a timber company for a large profit.

One lifelong resident of the Eureka area, Steven Puter, was especially adept at swindling on several levels. Puter had worked as a logger in the forests around Humboldt Bay, and he soon developed a side business of locating unclaimed property and selling the claims to newly arrived emigrants for $25.00. He charged another $25.00 to build a rude cabin for the buyer, thus satisfying part of the legal homestead bargain. When these supposed settlers gained final title to the land, Puter sold it for them to a Eureka businessman, receiving a fee for his service. The lands were then sold in bigger tracts—at $25.00 per acre—to lumber companies.

The fraud became even more obvious when the Timber and Stone Act of 1878 opened new

Opposite: One of the homesteaders' cabins built so that settlers would qualify to own claims of rich virgin redwood forest in Humboldt County. This cabin probably was never occupied, but simply was part of the speculation in trees.

Below: Three choppers pausing for a photo as they make the undercut in a huge coast redwood in Humboldt County. Note that the men are standing on springboards set into the trunk of the tree.

sections of wooded lands to claimants. Puter stated that he had seen agents of speculating companies take as many as 25 sailors from a bar or boarding house in Eureka to file notices of intent to become United States citizens and then make claims on property in the forest. These sailors never turned up again, but their claims somehow later were deeded to the company that had paid for their trip to the filing office. A decade later, this wholesale fraud was curbed by a zealous federal agent, but by then millions of dollars in timber and thousands of acres of irreplaceable virgin trees were lost to legitimate settlers and to history.

Opposite: A remaining virgin stand in the coast redwood region, one of the relatively small proportion saved from the loggers' axes and saws.

Below: Three men would work 1 week to fell a tree this size; note the bark, which is at least 1 foot thick at the base, and the enormous cross-cut saw, which is too long for the camera's range.

EXHIBITIONISM

Right: The stripping of bark from the Mother of the Forest, in Calaveras Big Trees, in 1854. Speculator George Trask hired a crew to build scaffolding and strip the bark to a height of 116 feet; sections of this tree's protective layer were shipped to New York and London for exhibit. The tree stood, intact but dead, until a 1908 fire destroyed all but a snag of it.

DESCRIPTION OF THE
MAMMOTH TREE FROM CALIFORNIA,
NOW ERECTED AT THE
CRYSTAL PALACE, SYDENHAM,
PRICE, SIXPENCE.

Because of the difficulty of transporting timber in the mountainous terrain of the Sierra Nevada, the giant sequoias were less vulnerable to rampant exploitation by fraudulent claims, although some swindlers operated in the region. These monumental trees were subject to exploitation of another sort, however—their awesome size inspired many speculators to carve off sections of the huge trees and to put these specimens on display around the world, for a price, of course.

The impetus to commit such travesties as cutting down Big Trees or peeling off their bark was the international uproar that greeted the news of these giants' discovery. In addition to the botanists' squabbles over naming the trees, the popular reports of their size and age were so varied and occasionally so outrageous that the facts were often hard to recognize. One tree that was felled in the rush of enthusiasm to exhibit its parts was measured on the ground and its height reported as 450 feet, which no giant sequoia has ever approached. Other early accounts claimed that Big Trees were as tall as 600 feet and that they were capable of growing to heights of 1000 feet.

To settle the disparities and to turn a profit, a few enterprising pitchmen arranged to exhibit portions of Sierra redwoods so the world could see their true dimensions. The greatest travesty

of this kind was performed on the tallest tree left intact in the Calaveras Grove, 'Mother of the Forest,' as the local Indians had called it. George Trask, the perpetrator, was impatient of the time involved in felling such a giant—it stood 321 feet high—and eager to sidestep the expense of cutting and shipping sections of the tree. Thus, he hit upon a scheme to strip the bark from this tree and reassemble it for public viewing. In 1854 Trask hired a crew who drilled holes in the tree and placed supports in them for a huge scaffold, where the workers stood as they cut away the bark from the ground level to a height of 116 feet. This great assemblage of

Left: An 1855 photo of the Mother of the Forest, showing the marks where scaffolding was set into the tree's trunk.

the tree's protective layer was then hauled to Stockton, California, where it was put aboard a ship for the Pacific, and ultimately for New York and London.

The greedy Trask had cashed in on his novelty, which was displayed at the Crystal Palace in New York in 1855 and then in England's Crystal Palace until that building burned down in 1866. Yet his scheme had doomed a magnificent and unique specimen of nature. The Mother of the Forest died a slow death, deprived of protection and much of the sustenance for survival. The naked tree continued to stand until 1908, when a fire destroyed much of its foliage and trunk; a sorry remnant of the tree remains in the north Calaveras Grove today.

Below left: A cross section of a redwood on public display.

Opposite and below: Lithographs by Edward Vischer of the Calaveras Big Trees. Vischer's work was instrumental in spreading the fame of these magnificent trees around the world.

George Trask had learned how hard it was—and how costly—to cut down a large sequoia for display by observing the first attempt in one of the Calaveras groves in 1852. No saws were big enough to cut across the gigantic trunk of this tree, which stood 302 feet high and measured 96 feet in circumference at its base. So a crew of five men used augurs to bore large holes in the tree on all sides, as deep as the tools would penetrate. Then the crew drove wedges into the holes on one side of the tree, pounding the implements deeper by hanging logs on ropes from higher up on the trunk and swinging the logs against the wedges. This effort took 25 men 10 days, and still the tree did not move. After several more days of work, the job was finished not by the determined loggers, but by the wind—a gust blew the tree over when the crew was away from the site on a meal break. The trunk of this colossal tree was half-buried in the mud after its fall, and the crown had splintered into hundreds of jagged pieces.

Although some of the bark and trunk sections of this broken giant were sent off to exhibitions in San Francisco and New York, the stump of the first Big Tree felled by men became a center of attraction in the Calaveras groves. In 1854 a makeshift cotillion was fashioned on top of the stump, which had been evened off and its surface smoothed. On the Fourth of July a dancing party was held atop the stump, where 32 dancers, several musicians and a dozen observers shared the spacious floor. Two enterprising businessmen had already built a hotel near the fallen tree, and a bowling alley was constructed on top of the fallen sections of trunk that lay nearby.

Another glorious Sierra redwood was cut from a grove in King's Canyon for exhibition in 1891. This tree, named for Mark Twain, was reported to be 331 feet tall, had no sizable fire scars and was the most perfect specimen in its area. One cross-section of the Twain tree was

THE STUMP AND TRUNK OF THE MAMMOTH TREE OF CALAVERAS.

Showing a Cotillion Party of Thirty-two Persons Dancing on the Stump at one time

sent to the American Museum of Natural History in New York, and a second was given to the British Museum in London; both can still be seen today at these sites. The rest of this incomparable example of nature's perfection was cut up for grapestakes and fenceposts.

The coast redwoods, too, were celebrated publicly, often for the durability and usefulness of their wood as lumber. At the Columbian Exposition in Chicago in 1893, some 28 million people viewed 'the biggest plank ever sawed'; this single board measured 16 feet 5 inches in width and apparently contained a section of burl, for its grain was arranged in intricate patterns. In 1914 another Chicago exhibit featured a 60-year-old barn that was shipped intact from Humboldt County; visitors could enter the barn and see that it was still in perfect condition.

These fine timber trees were also the subject of both skeptical detracters and enthusiastic supporters in the nineteenth century. One such supporter was American business magnate William Waldorf Astor, who was challenged to back up his claim that the slab cut from a single redwood tree would make a table to seat 40 people for dinner. Astor had a cross-section cut from a virgin tree north of San Francisco, and a German ship carried the massive cargo to London for settlement of this wager. Astor was an easy winner: the 2-foot-thick table measured 16 feet 6 inches in diameter on the underside and 14 feet 11 inches in diameter on the top surface, and the circumference was 52 feet—easily enough room for 40 guests and silver place settings.

Not all who were fascinated by the discovery of California's redwoods approved of the exploitation of these trees, however. The editor of one popular magazine of the time, *Gleason's Pictorial Drawing Room Companion,* offered his opinion of the felling of the first giant sequoia in 1853: 'It seems a cruel idea, a perfect desecration, to cut down such a splendid tree,' this editor wrote. He suggested that in Europe such a tree would have been protected, by law if necessary, whereas in America 'the purchaser chops it down, and ships it off for a show!'

Opposite above: A lithograph of a party of 32 people dancing on the stump of the Discovery Tree—Dowd's original grizzly bear tree—in the North Calaveras Grove.

Left: Choppers working on their knees while making the undercut for felling the Mark Twain Tree. See pages 70–71 for a photo of this magnificent tree as it fell.

Opposite below: The General Noble Tree, of which a 30-foot section was displayed at the Columbian Exposition in Chicago in 1893. The section was later displayed at the Mall in Washington, DC, and subsequently taken to the US government's Arlington Experiment Farm, where it was 'misplaced.'

USING THE REDWOODS

Neither species of redwood tree was cut for mere novelty alone. While the Big Trees did yield to the greed of pitchmen when first discovered, the far greater value of both sequoias lay in their use as timber. At the time of the Spanish missions and the discovery of gold, the West was being settled by a hardy stock of frontiersmen, and the loggers among them saw these immense trees as a challenge to their strength and skill, rather than a natural treasure to be saved and protected.

The sheer size of the coast and Sierra redwoods invited their demise, even before the excellent qualities of their lumber (or at least of the coast tree's lumber) were known. The coast redwood was readily recognized as the easier tree to harvest, because of its proximity to rivers and coast harbors and because of its more 'shatterproof' quality when felled. Although the potential volume of a Sierra redwood is twice that of the largest coast tree, the huge percentage of waste —from 50 to 75 percent —in felling the Big Trees made them a much less efficient source of lumber. Thus, the Sierra redwoods had only a short reign as commercial timber and have not been cultivated for this purpose, as have coast redwoods. The average yield of an acre of old-growth *Sequoia sempervirens* is 125,000 to 150,000 board feet per forest acre, and some dense virgin stands have produced much more. The now-obliterated flat stands that fell to the logger's axe yielded 200,000 to 500,000 board feet per acre, and early records claim one yield of a million and a half board feet of lumber from a single acre of trees. One living tree in Humboldt County has the greatest estimated timber volume:

Opposite: A team of 14 oxen hauling a load of logs along a skid road in Mendocino County. They are at the landing, where the 14 logs of 12 to 20 feet each will be left for railroad pickup. This single load of trunk sections contains 6000 board feet of lumber.

if cut, it would supply 361,336 board feet of finished lumber, enough to make 22 five-room houses.

The same protective features that permit redwood trees to live so long and reach such immense size also enhance their value as lumber. The wood's absence of resin and the straightness of its grain make it workable and strong, and coast redwood has the least shrinkage of any softwood grown in North America. Like the trees themselves, the boards made from redwoods are resistant to fire—again, because of their lack of resin—and their sponginess enables them to soak up water readily if ignited. Both of these qualities make buildings of redwood less susceptible to fire than those made of pine, and one early champion of redwood lumber claimed that the city of San Francisco, chiefly composed of redwood structures, had no major fires until the 1906 earthquake aftermath, when water was unavailable to fight the raging blazes.

Coast redwoods have been found to contain two very specialized chemicals, sequirin A and B, that are unpalatable to insects and fungi. These substances protect the wood when it is lumber as well, and one of the principal uses of sequoia is in the underpinning of structures and in decks, fences and other ground-contact locations. Although giant sequoias have not been tested for these substances, the Big Trees' resistance to pests suggests that their wood also contains such chemical protection.

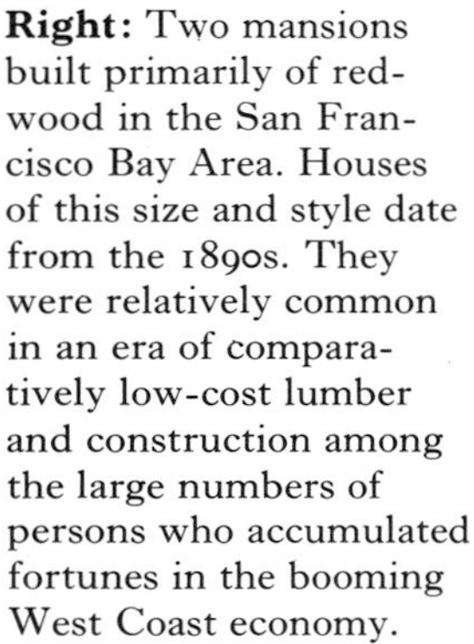

Right: Two mansions built primarily of redwood in the San Francisco Bay Area. Houses of this size and style date from the 1890s. They were relatively common in an era of comparatively low-cost lumber and construction among the large numbers of persons who accumulated fortunes in the booming West Coast economy.

EARLY LOGGING

THE LOGGERS WHO FELLED THAT FIRST GIANT SEQUOIA in one of the two Calaveras groves could not make their saws or axes do the job. In the coastal forests, where the trees were less formidable in width, persistent choppers with sharp axes could open large enough undercuts to make room for saws, although this process often required three to five days. However, men with axes and saws were only a small part of the logging team in a redwood forest.

The logging camps were home for hundreds of men, who worked a forest for nine or 10 months of each year, retreating from their outdoor habitats when the rain and mud became constant. The men who fought and conquered these living towers were mostly veterans of forests in Maine or Nova Scotia, and many were Europeans who had not given up their native languages, which resulted in a noisy mixture of tongues and a wide choice of swearwords in these rough-speaking bachelor domains.

Each logging crew had about a dozen men whose duties were as strictly delineated as any cluster of labor unions could wish. The chopping boss, often called the bull buck, determined which trees would be cut and in what order, assigning the teams to a strip they would work for four weeks or more. The choppers, or fellers, actually cut down the tree, but a great deal of preparation went into their task. These two experts were armed with a pair of axes, 8-foot saws, a 12-foot saw and various wedges

Left: Scenes of the early loggers at work transporting logs for storage at the mill pond; making an undercut; and loading trunk sections at the railhead.

Right: Conventional cross-cut saws were not nearly big enough to tackle giant sequoias such as this one, intended for a World's Fair. This tree in Mammoth Grove was 99 feet in circumference and 312 feet tall.

Below: About felling coast redwoods, one of the loggers' sayings was, 'cut 'em high to lay 'em low.' The choppers worked high up on the trunk to avoid cutting through the wider base of the tree.

and plates. Perhaps their most crucial tool was the smallest one—a plumb bob, with which they gauged whether the tree was straight or a 'leaner' and where it would fall.

Once the path of the falling tree had been determined, several crew members prepared a bed for it by toppling small trees and boughs in its path to cushion the fall. Unless a tree was leaning in some other direction, the fellers always tried to guide it for an uphill fall, because it was likely to do less damage to its own trunk and to nearby trees on this shorter fall.

When the bed was laid, the choppers went to work. They built a platform to stand on or put 'springboards' into the trunk several feet off the ground, to avoid having to cut through the wider base. After a large V-shaped section was chopped away, the two choppers finished their job with a cross-cut saw, occasionally using dynamite to topple an especially unyielding tree.

If the tree fell the wrong way or was damaged badly, the loggers usually left it and went on to the next redwood, wasting a virgin life as well as thousands of feet of usable wood. Despite the fellers' skill and experience, some trees got away from them, at times wrecking numerous other trees and maiming crew members or animals that could not get clear in time.

Once a tree was felled, the 'buckers' sawed it into manageable lengths, usually 32 feet each.

Left: The remains of the original Russian sawmill at Fort Ross, as it appeared in the 1890s.

Below: A logging camp in the Sierra Nevada Mountains, 1884. Run as a cooperative venture by its members, this enterprise lasted only seven years.

Loggers strike a casual pose beside a fallen virgin coast redwood near Fort Bragg. They are cutting it into 24-foot sections for transport to the sawmill.

Right: The sections of some of the largest giant sequoias had to be blasted in half with dynamite before ox teams could haul them out of the forest. This photo shows a blasting crew in 1888.

Below: Ox teams hauling small loads to the head of a skid road in Sonoma County.

These men also removed the branches, and then 'barkers' peeled away the bark with long poles. Next came one of the most dangerous tasks—rolling the logs within reach of the teams of oxen that would haul them out of the forest. The men who rolled the giant logs were called 'jackscrewers'; they used jacks and peaveys to turn the logs over and start them rolling toward the staging area, which was always downhill—preferably at a gentle grade—from the felling site.

When all the logs had been hauled away from the cutting area, the loggers would burn the unwanted branches, splinters and accompanying undergrowth. This left a constant pall of smoke over some forests, and it added to the look and smell of destruction in the region. Yet nature's regenerative powers were stronger than the axes and fires, and in a few weeks new seedlings had taken hold in the desolate, treeless patches. In fact, such burning helped the redwood trees to sprout, for it cleansed the soil for them.

Before any mechanized systems were invented for hauling logs, teams of oxen, or occasionally horses, were used to pull the huge loads. As many as 16 animals would be yoked together in pairs along a chain that had been wrapped around several logs, the largest weighing up to 20 tons. The 'bullwhacker' would drive the animals along a 'skid road,' which had been made of uniform-sized logs laid crosswise. This skid system prevented the newly cut logs from sinking into the soft earth or snagging on rocks and trees. To control the friction-induced heat on the skid road, as well as to keep the load sliding, one of the lowly members of the crew—often a young boy or a Chinese laborer—would throw water on the skid logs behind the animals and in front of the logs. The 'chain-tender' rode atop the logs being hauled to make certain that the water carrier kept the skids wet and that the chains held their load evenly and securely.

This primitive transportation method required that the groves of trees cut and pulled from the forest be located fairly near a landing, such as a river bank or flume. Often a box flume was built to carry the stripped logs from the forest site to a lake or river; the flume was a wooden aqueduct of sorts, a three-sided channel filled with just enough water to keep a log floating. Flumes served as a practical route for sending logs down steep hills to a waiting body of water, and the loads, weighing 10 tons or more, made a terrific splash at the end of their ride.

Most of the early sawmills were built along rivers and near a good ocean harbor, so that logs could be transported easily to the mill and lumber could be shipped out just as easily. The logs that had been cut and rolled or sent down a flume into a river would usually stay in place

Following pages: The reconstructed Mendocino Lumber Company mill on Big River in the 1860s. The original building was destroyed by fire, a common hazard in the lumber-making industry.

Below: Hillside logging area near the northern California coast, where logs were sent to the mill via flumes filled with water.

until the winter rains swelled the stream. The logging crew could control the movements of their huge jam of logs by building a dam or barrier in the river, opening it only when the conditions were right for a clean flow to the mill and when the mill pond had room for a new crop. The very weather that favored the growth of these huge virgin redwoods could cause great havoc with the river-based transport system, though; if too much weight built up behind a barrier, the force of the logs or the flooding river might tear the logjam loose and send it plummeting out of control toward the mill. Such violent parades tore up the river banks and flattened the growth near them, and much of the floating timber was damaged in the frantic flow.

Below: The China Grade Mill in the Big Basin area. From the number of standing trees near the mill, it appears this operation was just beginning to harvest and produce lumber at the time this photograph was taken.

THE MACHINE OF THE FOREST

In 1881 John Dolbeer, a mill owner and old-time logger in the Eureka area, built a steam-powered machine that put the bullwhackers out of business. Called the 'Dolbeer Donkey,' this odd-looking contraption had an upright steam boiler, a one-cylinder engine and a winding drum that carried steel cable or rope as a winch does. This machine would be hauled to the site where a felled tree was to be pulled out of the grove; then the cable would be secured around the logs and the engine given full power, turning the drum and pulling the logs along the skid road faster than the most efficient team of animals. In short order the loggers became aware that skid roads too were no longer needed with such a powerful pulling machine, and the Dolbeer invention resulted in far greater destruction of the forest environment than the clumsy old process had.

At the same time, the newly completed railroads in the northern California woodlands replaced many of the flumes and logjams. A railroad siding could be extended more easily to remote locations than the skid roads or water-dependent routes, and the steam donkey could haul logs onto waiting flatcars. The owners of sawmills, too, benefitted from the railroads,

Left and below: The old and new methods of hauling logs in the 1800s The Dolbeer Donkey, shown below, was an important innovation in logging, although its use was often harder on the terrain than the old skid road method.

Opposite: Tracks of the Northwestern Pacific Railroad passing through a redwood grove near the Eel River in northern California. Only one line of this once-extensive log-hauling network still runs —from Eureka southwest to the town of Willits.

Right: Another steam donkey, in the foreground; a truck fitted with rail-riding wheels, in the background, was used as a switch engine for loads of timber at Caspar in Mendocino County.

Right: Running Big Tree logs into the mill at Converse Basin in the Sierra mountains. The logs are pulled along a wooden track by a Dolbeer steam donkey, at right in background.

often building extensive networks of track to carry logs and lumber to various parts of the yard, as well as to distant parts of the continent. By the early 1900s, the oxen had been replaced by mechanical donkeys, and in 1914 the railroad link between Sausalito (just north of the Golden Gate) and Eureka, the principal logging center, was finished.

Modern machines invaded the redwoods in the 1930s, when tractors came into wide use for hauling logs. The big 'cats'—a nickname for their most prolific manufacturer, Caterpillar Tractor Company—could cut roads to the logging sites, climb nearly vertical hills to pluck choice trees from the forest, and haul logs to staging areas or the backwoods sawmills that prospered in the 1940s and 1950s. The choppers' axes and hand saws were replaced by gas-powered chain saws, and gleaming logging trucks began to thunder down the dirt logging roads and the region's highways carrying several tons of timber. Today the machines in use have become diversified; thus, a 'cat' can haul logs, lift them onto a truck, cut and grade a road and

Opposite: Workers of the Hammond Lumber Company, in Humboldt County, showing off the climbing ability of the logging cruiser in 1928. The cruiser was an early version of the caterpillar-type tractors used for logging today.

Right: A steam-powered saw for cutting trunks into sections in a photo from 1923.

Below: Trainloads of logs on trunk lines at the Excelsior Redwood Company in Eureka.

Preceding pages: A steam traction engine at work in Mendocino County in the early 1920s. These powerful machines were used to haul heavy loads for short distances in the level areas of logging camps and sawmill yards.

Right: The modern 'cat,' an extremely versatile machine for hauling and lifting heavy loads and covering virtually any terrain. Its impact on the forests has been significant both in terms of damage to the land and in opening up heretofore 'un-loggable' sites.

even dig a hole.

The sawmills at the forest's edge gained in mechanical sophistication from their water-powered beginnings, but their processes have not changed appreciably from the mid-nineteenth century to the present. Logs are brought from the mill pond or from the yard into the main building of a mill, where the huge saws rip them into thick boards. These crude boards are carried on rollers to an array of additional saws and planes, which cut and smooth the wood to prescribed sizes. The mill's conveyor system sorts the different-sized pieces of lumber and carries them to the appropriate storage areas. The finished lumber is stacked outside in the mill's spacious yard, as are huge piles of logs waiting to be cut. Railroad cars and large trucks are ever present in the yard, delivering new fodder for the saws and taking away the lumber for sale. The ships that were so prevalent a century ago no longer call at the mills, but in their heyday, they lined up in wait for redwood cargo. In 1876, at least 1100 ships called at Humboldt Bay to carry 'sequoia gold' to such far-flung destinations as Australia, India, Hawaii and South Africa.

Left: The bark *Kobenhaven* unloading redwood lumber at a manufacturing plant in the San Francisco Bay Area, 1923.

Below: A beached lumber schooner along the Mendocino County coast; beaching was a common occurrence in the heyday of lumber hauling by ship.

A CENTURY OF LOGGING

ALTHOUGH NEVER SO PERSISTENT AS THE COASTAL LOGGING, the cutting of Sierra redwoods for lumber consumed 34 percent of their total acreage. Only one major grove was virtually obliterated; this was the Converse Basin, which covered some 2600 acres. The one remaining old-growth tree in this southern Sierra location is the third largest of the giant sequoias—the Boole Tree, named for Frank Boole, who was foreman of the logging operation in Converse Basin and who decided to spare this one tree. The loggers were aided in this generous decision by the fact that the tree stands on a rocky hillside, meaning that this unusually large specimen would almost certainly be splintered beyond use or recognition when it fell. Their tendency to shatter, in fact, saved many enclaves of Sierra redwoods from exploitation as timber.

The statistics of logging history in the *Sequoia sempervirens* forests are much grimmer. More than one-third of the original virgin redwood forest was consumed by loggers and sawmills between 1850 and 1925, and yearly consumption increased after that time (except during the Depression and World War II). Mills and houses and sundecks and even pencils gobbled up the forests at a rate of 400 million to 600 million board feet each year since 1900, and the postwar building boom saw the redwood cutting reach 1 billion board feet in the early 1950s. The sawmills in the coastal region multiplied from 117 in 1945 to 229 in 1947 and to 398 in 1948. These lumber factories did not cut redwood timber alone, but sequoias remained the greatest part of their diet.

Opposite: An example of clearcutting from the 1960s. Scenes such as this helped to rally sentiment in favor of establishing a sizable Redwood National Park, and imposing stricter controls over logging practices.

Right: The Boole Tree, the one major giant sequoia spared during the logging of Converse Basin. Many trees cut here shattered on the rocky ground of the site.

Far right: A 1915 advertisement promoting the aesthetic and practical features of redwood products.

THE FUTURE OF THE FORESTS

Perhaps the most telling statistics are the predictions of future yields for the redwood forests. None are predicted for the giant sequoia, of course, for these trees are entirely protected (and a poor timber crop, anyway). From 1953 through 1976, annual coast redwood cutting remained steady at about 1 billion board feet per year. In 1970, about 150,000 acres of old-growth redwoods existed on private lands that would yield 14 billion board feet of lumber. As of 1976, this 'crop' had been reduced by cutting and by acquisition of parklands to 8 billion board feet, on about 85,000 acres of commercial property. In 1960 the United States Forest Service predicted that virtually all the virgin redwood timber would be consumed by 1980, if cutting continued at the rate prevailing then. Environmental constraints and selective logging have slowed the process somewhat, and now the prospect is that the tallest trees on private land will be gone by 1984.

Humboldt County, California, supplies 40

Right: The Redwood Manufacturers Company truck in a 1915 photo. The house on the back is advertising 'wavewood,' an uncommon form of coast redwood with a wavy grain.

Below: Pacific Lumber Company and its company-owned town of Scotia, in northwestern California. Little has changed in Scotia since this photo was taken in 1932, except that a new highway passes through to the right.

percent of the redwood lumber processed today. The rate of cutting there is more than twice the rate of growth for new redwoods; in short, an industry is killing itself, along with the virgin trees left to it. Some timber companies are cutting selectively and cutting less, and a few have managed to achieve a balance between new growth and trees cut. In general, however, forest management has not taken adequate note of the future, particularly in regard to trees that take 2000 years to grow and less than two hours to fell with a long-armed chain saw.

Equally sobering is the prospect for second-growth logging. Although the fast-maturing *Sequoia sempervirens* can grow to 100 or even 200 feet tall and 6 feet in diameter in 60 years, its wood does not have the ideal timber properties of the vanishing virgin trees. Even second-growth trees that are 100 to 125 years old produce inferior lumber by old-growth standards—the wood is not as workable or as resistant to disease, insects or decay.

One factor making recent-growth redwood timber less desirable is the modern logging practice. Although the 17-ton tractors that make roads and haul trees can leave more large trees standing around their quarry than did the old steam donkeys and skid roads, the use of heavy machinery has affected the soil where new sequoias sprout. According to Dr. Richard

Far left: Logs being moved from the huge Scotia mill pond to a special processing plant.

Left: Finished lumber being loaded for rail shipment at Eureka.

Below left: A log being hauled up the track conveyor from the mill pond to the processing plant (below).

Following pages: Burning slash in a clearcut area of Humboldt County, 1972.

St. Barbe Baker, founder of The Men of the Trees, an international organization dedicated to conservation and land reclamation through tree planting, and a specialist in forest ecology, the engine vibrations of the huge 'cats' cause the soil to form a hardpan about 10 inches below the surface. This packing down of the soil prevents water from penetrating properly and also stifles the growth of young trees' roots. Although this situation has yet to be sufficiently studied, Baker predicts that the altered soil condition will drastically shorten the lifespan of second- and third-growth redwoods, perhaps to as little as 30 or 40 years.

The direction of redwood timber production and logging has been the subject of great controversy in the last few decades. Conservationists have long called for strong curbs on the careless practices of some timber harvesters, citing evidence of widespread damage to the forest environment at the logging site and for many miles around it. The lumber industry has opposed strict regulation by all levels of government, arguing that where logging occurs the livelihood of a region is dependent on continued logging and sawmill operations.

The state of California has been far-sighted in passing legislation to attempt regulation of the timber industry's practices, beginning with the Forest Practice Act of 1945. This law owed much of its content to the wishes of timber

Opposite: Another clear-cut area, with a token survivor. This remaining tree is a spiketop: much of its timber volume is lost, which may well account for its being left standing.

Right: A coast redwood tree farm, one of the timber industry's efforts to maintain a steady supply of redwood for construction through carefully managed forest preserves.

Below: Protected trees and harvested ones.

producers, however, and was declared unconstitutional in 1971 because its provisions amounted to legalized self-regulation by the industry. A new Forest Practice Act was passed in 1973, and this measure seems to have represented in a more balanced fashion the interests of both the conservationists and the logging industry. In practice, however, the environmental and aesthetic constraints written into the law have been largely overruled in favor of practical economics.

Unfortunately, the practical economics of a timber region whose chief crop is nearly exhausted are promising for neither the loggers nor the conservationists. The citizens' right to maintain the health of public forests and parklands, which are often affected by nearby logging in commercial old-growth stands, has been championed eloquently in the halls of the state legislature and the nation's capital. Yet these lawmakers cannot ignore the pleas of an industry that is suffering from self-inflicted wounds, particularly when the symbols of that ailment are parades of 'cats' and logging trucks in front of the capitol building.

Above right: Clearing the path to fell the tree at right. **Right:** Making the crosscut. **Far right:** The fallen tree from ground level. This tree fell exactly as the crew had planned.

Above: Hauling logs out of a cutting area on a specially built logging road. Many such roads crisscross the private and public lands of northern California's redwood forests, including some areas of the National Forests where timber cutting is still permitted.

Left: Sign near Redwood National Park advertising the lumber industry's point of view, which is not shared by conservationists.

BUILDING WITH REDWOODS

Opposite: The Carson House in Eureka is framed mostly of redwood, though its interior decor borrows from many European traditions rather than from the more rustic style of redwood finishing that became popular later.

Below: The 'House of Hoo-Hoo,' designed by architect Bernard Maybeck and built by the Pacific Lumbermen's Association for the Panama-Pacific Exposition in San Francisco in 1915. This highly unusual building utilizes sections of virgin redwood.

WHATEVER THE FUTURE YIELDS OF REDWOOD TIMBER, this tree is likely to remain a favorite for all types of construction. Most of California's wood-aged wine is stored in redwood tanks, and some liquor is also aged in redwood. Football fans at major colleges sit on redwood bleachers—in stadiums at the Universities of Michigan, Virginia, Iowa and Pittsburgh and Stanford University. Baseball fans were not forgotten, either, for the American League parks in Chicago and Boston have redwood seats.

The strength and relative lightness of redwood make it extremely useful for framing a building; its durability and high paint-retention qualities make it equally useful for siding, panelling and trim. Most of these general construction uses are concentrated in North America, with the greatest consumption of redwood timber occurring in California. Redwood is sold abroad for specialized purposes, for example as railroad ties, used extensively in Peru and South Africa. Many of the South African mine timbers are also redwood, because of the wood's special resistance to decay and pests.

In the past the bark of coast redwood trees traditionally had many uses, although today the cost of manufacturing products from it has become prohibitive. Like the lumber it once surrounded, redwood bark lasts indefinitely, and many people still benefit from products made with it decades ago. For example, the tough, spongy fibers of redwood bark were laid beneath the running tracks of many schools and athletic fields; it has served as insulation for electric water heaters, fur storage vaults and iceboxes, and it has been used as a sound-deadening filler in noisy environments.

As conventional insulation for the walls of a home, processed redwood bark has the same R values (insulating capacity according to thickness) as the more widely used fiberglas. One Nevada City, California, couple recently confirmed the utility of redwood-bark insulation when they began remodeling an old creamery as their home. The creamery building, which was built in the 1890s, had a walk-in cooler for storage of the dairy products; when the couple tore out the thick interior walls of this room, they removed a total of 300 10-gallon bags of Palco Wool, the trade name for redwood-bark insulation. The insulation material was completely undamaged, and the couple installed it in the roof of their 3400-square-foot converted

1▲

(1) Bags of redwood soil conditioner behind a young coast redwood seedling. (2) A young redwood tree beside a redwood water tank. (3) A cabin built of redwood on an old-growth redwood stump. (4) The 'One-Log House,' a commercial venture on Redwood Highway. (5) A school building constructed with redwood plywood. (6) A handmade house of recycled redwood lumber. (7) Natural redwood interior paneling in a contemporary California home.

2▲

3▲

4▲ 6▼

5▲ 7▼

Left: A redwood-shingled house among the coast redwoods. The sunshine here is somewhat misleading; for much of the year these woods are dark and damp, so that homes in redwood groves tend to remain perpetually cool, and often are a bit wet.

No. 91.

creamery.

From the first logging days, redwood has had its special champions—builders and designers who prized the functional qualities and the beauty of this lumber. Many of the great mansions of San Francisco were built entirely of redwood, although few of these structures survived the 1906 earthquake and fire and the later push of commercial progress. Two of the more prominent names of nineteenth-century California are associated with elegant redwood mansions—Leland Stanford, whose home was a stolid, square-pillored structure with a widow's walk at the top, and Mark Hopkins, whose many-gabled and turreted home gave way to the Nob Hill hotel that bears his name.

One turn-of-the-century California architect is closely associated with both redwood trees and redwood buildings. Bernard Maybeck, who designed 150 homes in the Berkeley and San Francisco area as well as some monumental civic buildings, used redwood for basic construction and rustic or formal decoration. Maybeck instituted several principles in house design that have become standards of much modern building, such as exposed beams and vertical members and trim, siding, and panelling of natural redwood. The architect is studied and revered as a pioneer in handsome, functional building, and the Maybeck homes that still stand (many have burned) are lovingly protected.

In 1903 Maybeck designed a small building that effectively marries redwood timber and forest. This is the clubhouse in a redwood grove belonging to the Bohemian Club of San Francisco, of which the architect was a member. This low, bungalow-style building sits unassumingly amid a dozen or more virgin redwoods, achieving the harmony of site and structure that is reminiscent of a Japanese temple. This building is subordinate to its forest surroundings, yet its hilltop setting commands a lovely view.

Opposite: The Maybeck-designed clubhouse for the Bohemian Club, located in Sonoma County on the Russian River.

Below: A Tudor-style home designed by Maybeck in San Francisco in 1909. This structure was built almost entirely of redwood.

CULTIVATED REDWOODS

SINCE THEIR BEAUTY AND UTILITY have become widely appreciated, it is not surprising that redwoods are being cultivated as both cash timber crops and decorative trees. The value of raising recent-growth sequoias as lumber-producing trees is yet to be thoroughly assessed, at least in comparison with using old-growth timber, but a number of commercial firms and forestry experts are working to design bigger and better redwood trees.

More than 600,000 acres of northern California land have been devoted to redwood tree farms, which are sanctioned by the commercial timber association. The managers of these forests pledge to use good forest practices in growing and harvesting the crops, including cutting timber in such a way that further growth is encouraged. To date, however, little effective regulation has been imposed on these tree farms, and their rate of cutting continues to exceed their rate of growth.

One practice in forest crop management that is potentially more alarming is the experimentation with redwood embryology to develop trees that are genetically appropriate for timber production. The hoped-for specimens would be fast-growing, and have straight trunks and few limbs. Yet the effects of such gene manipulation will not be seen for many years, and the breeding of a species whose virgin stock is

Opposite: A giant sequoia in the verdant English parklands. This isolated tree has grown to a height of 125 feet since it was planted in the late 1840s.

Left: Redwood sprouts on a stump one year after the parent tree was cut down.

Below: The exotically planted gardens at Stourhead in Wiltshire, England, showing maturing sequoias (both coast and giant) on the far side of the artificial lake.

shrinking rapidly could backfire. Dr. Rudolf Becking, a redwood expert, fears that such species engineering could damage the natural balance of the redwood forest, and he observes that the long-term results of such monocultural practices in food production have reduced the quality of the soil, the food being grown and the gene pool of the entire species.

Fortunately, the stands of protected virgin redwoods in parklands will continue to regenerate for the sake of the species and for the enrichment of all who see them. These mammoth sequoias will grow as natives only in their California habitat (and two small groves in Oregon), but the three sequoia species—coast, Sierra and dawn redwood—have been propagated all over the world, and some varieties that were developed in British and European nurseries do not grow in the trees' North American home.

The British have long been known for their cultivation of a great variety of trees, and the Scots are particularly adept at developing thriving adaptations of timber trees. The first redwood known to have been grown successfully outside North America, in fact, was planted at Smeaton-Hepburn in East Lothian, Scotland. This tree, a *Sequoia sempervirens,* was planted in 1844, and another coast redwood seedling was planted at Dropmore in Buckinghamshire the next year, to become England's first redwood. These early specimens were followed by similar plantings in estates and parks throughout Great Britain, primarily for decorative purposes but in some places as the beginnings of hoped-for timber crops.

In the mid-1850s, about a decade after the first redwood planting, the craze for Big Trees hit Britain. One early account of the Sierra redwood's journey to England relates that Pony Express riders carried a 2-ounce packet of giant sequoia seeds in a snuff box across the United States, at a cost of $25.00, sometime between 1846 and 1853. Some of these seeds were sprouted for seedlings in a Rochester, New York, nursery, and others made their way by ship to England. When the British botanist Lindley published his description and proposed name for the giant sequoia—*Wellingtonia gigantea*—in 1853, this tree's popularity exploded. These trees have since been so widely planted by the British that one member of the Royal Forestry Commission recently observed that 'there is scarcely a hilltop or mountain in all of Great Britain from which a giant sequoia cannot be seen.'

The giant sequoia seems particularly well adapted to the climate of the British Isles, and this tree grows taller and faster than most native species in both Britain and Europe. Despite this record of good growth, however, neither of the native North American sequoias has become a crop tree in England or Europe to any extent,

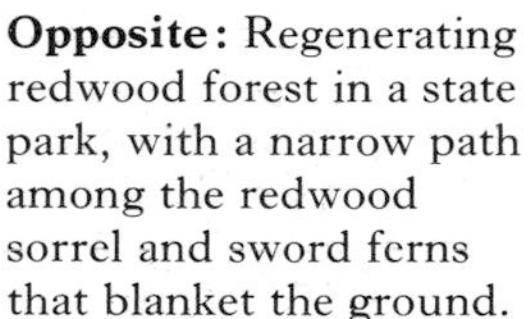

Opposite: Regenerating redwood forest in a state park, with a narrow path among the redwood sorrel and sword ferns that blanket the ground.

Left: Examples of coast redwoods that have been damaged by extreme weather conditions. At left, two trees show the effects of insufficient moisture, their tops burned and bare; at right, the continuous coastal winds prevented this seedling from getting vigorously established.

probably because the young trees of both species are susceptible to damage or death from frost in the areas where the climate otherwise permits their growth as mature trees. The hardier of the two, the giant sequoia, is also less desirable for timber because of its tendency to shatter when felled.

Several unusual varieties of sequoias are grown as decorative trees, however. The rarest of these is the pygmy variety of giant sequoia, which was developed in France and has been planted singly or in hedgerows in Britain and elsewhere. This tiny tree is only 5 to 6 inches tall at five years of age. Another odd variety of giant sequoia is the weeping sequoia, also developed in France. One large specimen of this tree is in the Trianon gardens at Versailles; another 75-foot weeping sequoia grows in the grounds of Inverary Castle in Scotland; and the most bizarre example of this tree—called 'the ugliest tree in Britain'—is found in Wales. At least one of these weeping trees is flourishing in the United States, on the campus of Stanford University in Palo Alto, California.

Yet another, less unusual sequoia variety is the *aureum,* which was developed in Ireland in 1856. It is characterized by golden yellow foliage but otherwise resembles the shape and size of its giant sequoia relatives. One of the largest of this species is found in Gloustershire, reaching a height of nearly 70 feet.

Redwood trees are also well represented on the European continent, even though the Ice Age drove out the original sequoia forests so that no continuous populations of sequoia survived there. The first redwoods in Europe were probably planted in Spain, simply because the Spanish explorers found and named the coast redwoods and are likely to have taken seeds of the tree back to their homeland. No living specimens of sequoia in Spain date from the explorers' time, though. The oldest sequoias of both species are located near Granada in southern Spain, where a small Sierra redwood forest is thriving and where several lovely coast redwoods may be found in the Garden of Generalife.

Much of France is too cold for the coast redwood, with the result that surviving specimens often lose their foliage in winter. One tree that was frozen and died back to ground level in the harsh winter of 1870 later sprouted and grew to a height of 50 feet; other trees in that same winter succumbed to the cold and did not regenerate. In warmer areas of France, coast redwoods have reached 100 feet or more in height, and one imposing avenue of these trees contains 50 trees about 100 feet tall and about 10 feet in diameter. The giant sequoia has fared much better in the French climate, growing to heights of 140 feet; at least 20 specimens in France are taller than 120 feet.

Sierra redwoods also prosper in Germany,

Right: Weeping sequoia, a variety of giant sequoia, has no typical form. This tree has been called 'the ugliest tree in Britain.'

Far right: The giant sequoia planted at La Granja, Spain. The largest sequoias in Europe, and possibly the largest trees there, they were planted in the 1880s and have reached diameters of 10 and 13 feet—a faster rate of growth than many Big Trees achieve in the Sierra Nevada.

which has the greatest number of imported redwoods in Europe. One German report claims that a tree that still stands at Oldenburg was grown from the early crop of seeds brought to England from California by English collector William Lobb. Supposedly Lobb gave some seeds to Lindley, who passed along samples to German naturalist Alexander von Humboldt; the latter raised a seedling for two years and then planted the young tree in 1858. Although coast redwoods do not grow well in Germany, Big Trees are found in many parks and dominate an experimental forest of American trees in the village of Weinheim on the Rhine River.

Because of the severe winters in the Scandinavian countries, both species of sequoia have difficulty surviving, although some Sierra redwoods have reached rather unspectacular heights of 65 to 70 feet in Norway and Denmark. Scattered specimens of Big Trees grow more heartily in Austria (a 90-foot tree grows in Vienna), Switzerland (where two coast redwoods have reached 80 years of age), Czechoslovakia, Belgium and Romania.

The coast redwood seems to flourish in northern Italy, where the largest European specimen can be found at Isola Madre in Lake Maggiore. This tree is about 120 years old and at least 130 feet tall. Other *Sequoia sempervirens* are found near Rome and Naples, and a few giant sequoias are growing near Florence.

In parts of the world where conifers are not native, such as South Africa, Australia and New Zealand, redwood propagation has been tried in an effort to cultivate a tree crop. The South African experiments have been unsuccessful, although other North American conifers are grown there for timber.

Australia has much native hardwood but little coniferous softwood, and many cutover hardwood forests have been replanted in the two main species of sequoia. Neither redwood has proved successful there as a timber tree, however; in most areas the giant sequoia cannot live more than 40 to 50 years in the comparatively dry Australian climate, and the coast redwood grows poorly as well (though it usually fares better than the Sierra tree). Both trees are widely planted as decorative species, however, growing to less than 100 feet high in most places. The tallest specimens of both redwoods are located mainly in Victoria, Queensland, and South Australia, in areas where rainfall reaches about 40 inches per year.

The climate of New Zealand is more hospitable to both North American sequoias, particularly on the North Island of this nation. A 15-acre grove of coast redwoods was planted near the town of Rotorua in 1901; its trees were pruned to a height of 50 feet in 1939, and since then the tallest specimens have grown to heights of 170 to 185 feet. This redwood grove is part of

Left: Coast redwoods are planted as popular urban and suburban landscaping trees within the coastal fogbelt. At left, the 3-year-old specimens are already eight feet tall; they have been mulched with shredded redwood bark.

the 18,000-acre Whakarewarewa National Forest, which is a primary research station for timber crop trees, as well as a popular recreational area in New Zealand. The redwood grove is not intended for use as future lumber, though—it was dedicated in 1947 as a memorial to all members of the New Zealand Forest Service who died in the two world wars.

Although less common in the timber-growing region of New Zealand, one excellent specimen of giant sequoia is located near the town post office in Rotorua. This tree is the local Christmas tree and is strung with lights for the holiday season each year. The fact that this Sierra redwood has been chosen for such a tradition is indicative of its beauty and stature in the principal timber-growing region of New Zealand.

Right: The weeping coast redwood, or Pendula, in Rotorua, New Zealand.

Far right: The redwood forest reaching down to the oceanside in Humboldt County, California—a landscape remarkably similar to parts of New Zealand's.

Because New Zealand's climate favors the growth of native North American conifers such as redwoods, several large plantations were planted in *Sequoia sempervirens* early in the twentieth century. Based on the popularity of virgin redwood lumber imported from California and the relatively fast growth of these trees in New Zealand, tree farmers anticipated a profitable forest crop, but the cultivated redwoods did not reach their potential either in size or in utility as timber. Apparently the fast growth encouraged by the commercial farmers and the lack of growers' attention to the trees as young seedlings resulted in timber that tends to shatter (like the Sierra redwood in California) when felled and lumber that lacks the strength and resistance to disease that characterize its North American counterpart. Consequently redwoods are ornamental trees in New Zealand, although the government forestry service continues to research ways of adapting them for future growth as timber.

Coast redwood trees have been propagated in Japan and China, along with renewed plantings of the metasequoia. The Sierra redwood has been less successfully grown in Asia, partly because of its susceptibility to a disease that originates with the Japanese *Cryptomeria,* a genus of the same family as sequoias.

Coast redwood trees have also been grown in tropical areas, such as plantations on the Hawaiian islands of Maui, Kauai and Oahu. Specimens planted in 1927 have grown to more than 100 feet in height; some of the larger trees have been harvested for their timber, although this was not the original intention of the planters. Coastal sequoias in Mexico City have likewise reached heights of 100 feet or more in 60 years of growth. Both the coast and Sierra redwoods have been grown experimentally in Brazil, and coast trees also thrive in small numbers in Argentina and Uruguay.

On their native continent, both species of sequoias have been cultivated as decorative trees throughout the United States and Canada. The northern parts of North America are generally too cold for the coast redwood, but giant sequoias thrive in numerous Canadian areas, as well as in the northeastern United States. These redwoods do not reach the sizes typical of their California habitat, however; the largest giant sequoia in the Eastern United States was less than 80 feet tall when measured in the 1960s.

The oldest and largest coast redwood on the Atlantic Coast has a notable history. This tree, located in Norfolk, Virginia, is said to have been planted as one of an avenue of redwoods by a Captain Weir. He brought a collection of seedlings from California by ship around Cape Horn in the 1850s for his eastern estate, but only one of the transplanted specimens survived. This tree now is more than 100 feet tall and approximately 4 feet in diameter.

All of these far-flung redwoods reflect the remarkable adaptability and staying power of the sequoia tree. Although the California parklands remain the only permanent home for virgin sequoias that date from times before Christ, the redwoods throughout the world are ever-graceful reminders of this magnificent breed of tree.

Below: Second-growth redwoods reappearing in a once heavily-logged area north of San Francisco, which is now a protected watershed for a Marin County reservoir.

Left: Shaped redwood trees on the grounds of a mansion in San Jose, 1910.

PROTECTING THE REDWOODS

Though the redwoods have long had their exploiters and profiteers, they have had protecters for even longer. The native Americans who lived among the coast and Sierra forests spoke for these trees with their actions, revering and often worshipping the marvels with which nature had surrounded them. Such an uncomplicated perspective has much to teach a modern society caught in the throes of commerce and technology. The opportunity all of us have to learn the lessons of nature is nowhere more splendid than in the stands of virgin sequoias that have been set aside for everyone's benefit.

A great variety of people have taken up the mantle of the Indians who left the native redwood forests undisturbed. In the modern world, protecting the trees has meant compromise and cooperation among many people, though a few outstanding individuals have gained public recognition for their efforts. Known and unknown, their campaign has been for the trees' survival, and ultimately their accomplishments will prove vastly more impressive and valuable than the feats of the daring choppers and bullwhackers.

Probably the best-known name associated with sequoias is John Muir, naturalist, writer, conservationist and founder and first president of the Sierra Club. Scotsman Muir, whose family moved to a Wisconsin farm when he was 11 years old, is most closely identified with the Sierra Nevada and Yosemite Valley, but his strong voice favored protection of all old-growth redwoods in California, and his stature as a conservationist enabled him to influence a President—among others—to create vast areas of national parks.

Opposite: A National Park Service erosion control project. The water ladder in the foreground drains excess runoff; in the back ground, willow wattle (willow shoots placed in small trenches) has been planted to hold the soil in place on a previously logged hillside.

Right: John Muir beside a woodland stream in the 1890s; below, on a Sierra Club outing in 1903.

Far right: Muir Woods, in a scene off the well-used main trails.

Below right: Beach and wild coastal headlands of Redwood National Park.

STATE AND NATIONAL PARKS

ALTHOUGH THE MARIPOSA GROVE of giant sequoias and Yosemite Valley had been made a state grant in 1864, before Muir's arrival in the West, he tirelessly explored and promoted these natural wonders. In 1889, Muir launched a campaign to create a Yosemite National Park, which was greatly aided by the naturalist's articles in Robert Underwood Johnson's *Century Magazine*. In 1890 a national park was created, but it included neither the valley nor the Mariposa Grove, which remained under the control of the state. Muir fervently believed that federal protection for these areas was preferable to state conservatorship, and he struggled for 16 years to win such protection, an effort that included, in 1892, the founding of the Sierra Club. Muir made numerous public speeches and lobbying trips to Sacramento to urge the legislature to cede these territories to the national park system. In 1905, the legislature passed this hotly contested measure, and in 1906 President Theodore Roosevelt signed the congressional bill accepting responsibility for some of the most spectacular scenery on earth.

Roosevelt himself was an outdoorsman of some repute, and an admirer of both John Muir and the giant sequoias of Muir's mountain domain. When he was governor of New York, Roosevelt had urged the federal government—unsuccessfully—to purchase the two Calaveras groves of Big Trees, and after he became president, he again worked to secure a congressional appropriation for this purpose. Finally, in 1909, Roosevelt signed into law a bill that established the North Grove of these trees as Calaveras Bigtree National Forest. During his presidency, he established five other national parks, 18 monuments, and 148 million acres of national forests.

During his years of championing a system of

Left: President Theodore Roosevelt and party on a visit to California to view several wilderness areas under consideration for federal protection.

national parks, Theodore Roosevelt visited much of the western wilderness, and in 1903 he took a trip to Yosemite Valley and had a sojourn with John Muir. Teddy took advantage of this opportunity to 'outskirt and keep away from civilization,' and instead of participating in the planned fireworks display and fancy-dress banquet, he joined Muir for a short camping trip. The President slept on an outdoor 'bed' of 40 old army blankets, ate a steak cooked over a campfire, and weathered a brief May snowstorm with his friend Muir.

For his part, John Muir used this rare occasion to speak for the wilderness, and Roosevelt listened. Muir is credited with assuring federal protection of two other important wilderness areas—the Grand Canyon and the Petrified

Below: Theodore Roosevelt (center) with John Muir (to his right) and others in Mariposa Grove during the President's 1903 visit to Yosemite Valley.

Forest of Arizona—as a result of his campfire chats with a President. The philosophy that John Muir expressed throughout his lifelong campaign for preserving nature's unique grandeur is aptly stated in one of his brief comments about the national parks: 'Thousands of nerve-shaken, overcivilized people are beginning to

Shall It Be This? **. . . Or This?**

find out that going to the mountains is going home; that wildness is a necessity; and that mountain parks and reservations are useful not only as fountains of timber and irrigating rivers, but as fountains of life.'

A great proportion of the giant sequoias were saved from logging through the reservation of the Calaveras and Mariposa groves. Meanwhile, protection of the immense groves to the south of Yosemite was being won by conservationists whose dedication equalled Muir's, and in 1890 (a month before creation of the Yosemite National Park), a federal law created Sequoia and General Grant National Parks; in 1940, the General Grant preserve became part of the larger King's Canyon National Park.

The public credit for creation of parks that protect and make accessible such natural wonders as the redwoods usually goes to the leaders, such as Muir, and the politicians who sponsor legislation and ride it through Congress.

Opposite: Spring runoff in Crescent Meadow of the Giant Forest in Sequoia National Park. At the turn of the century this fragile area was badly impacted from overgrazing by livestock.

Right: A cartoon by Ralph Yardley from the Stockton, California *Record*, 1928.

Below: An early tourist vehicle among the Big Trees in the 1930s.

Yet they would not have succeeded without the quiet efforts of millions of average citizens. Many legislative votes have been swayed in favor of acquiring redwood groves with public money by the earnest testimony and correspondence of these small-scale naturalists. In 1901, for example, the supporters of federal purchase of the Calaveras Big Trees sent President Roosevelt a petition signed by 1,437,260 people.

Nor were the redwoods without their somewhat eccentric defenders. One such man was Jesse Hoskins, a rancher from the San Joaquin Valley of southern California who spent many summers cutting fenceposts from fallen trees in the Sierra redwood groves. Hoskins became concerned that too much logging was being done in the unreserved sequoia groves, and in the 1890s he filed a homestead claim on 80 acres of the trees to protect them from being cut. To satisfy the requirement that he live on his claim, Hoskins carved out a room, 12 feet in diameter and 7 feet high, inside a partially burned but still-growing sequoia. To earn a living, the homesteader sold carvings made from the heartwood he had removed from the tree. Hoskins was successful in keeping the loggers away, and his tree home, which he named 'Hercules,' still stands.

The story of another man living in a hollow redwood tree provided the impetus for the first coast redwoods park. Legend had it that the famous explorer John C Fremont had once lived in a redwood in the virgin forest near Santa Cruz, California. When a local photographer, Andrew P Hill, went to the privately owned grove to photograph a forest fire (which was ultimately extinguished with the wine from a neighboring winery), he heard about this tree and decided to return to interview the owner of the property. In early 1900, Hill spoke with the owner, who was furious that the photographer had taken pictures in his grove, because he claimed exclusive rights to sell any such photos. This irascible man also told Hill that he intended to sell the timber in his stands of virgin redwoods, so nobody would see the legendary 'Fremont tree.'

The encounter angered and frustrated Hill, who had grown up among the coast redwoods and had been documenting the area's natural scenery for a number of years. Because Hill's photographs were used to illustrate newspaper articles and books about the San Jose and Santa Cruz areas, he knew a number of writers whom he could enlist in support of the cause he decided to champion—saving this grove of trees from the axe. Some northern California newspapers had previously editorialized in favor of establishing a redwoods park in the region, and these writers also joined the new crusade.

By the spring of 1900, public interest had grown significantly, and one supporter, the

Right: Photographer and conservationist Andrew P Hill next to the massive Father Tree in Big Basin State Park; at right, holding his well-known painting of this impressive tree.

president of Stanford University, invited all interested persons to a meeting in the campus library on 1 May. Amid the general enthusiasm for establishing a redwoods park, one botanist suggested that another stand of trees, the Big Basin forest, was far larger than the grove Hill had discovered, and the group's attention focused on Big Basin from then on. In a four-day exploration of the new area, Hill and eight other conservationists confirmed the reputation of this primeval forest, and they convinced a local sawmill owner whose crews were about to begin logging there to give them an option on 14,000 acres of this woodland, in the hope that they could buy it rather than see it cut. On their last night in the forest, this group of two women and seven men founded the Sempervirens Club, pledging their slim holdings of $32.00 to carry on the fight. The group decided to appeal to the California legislature to purchase the Big Basin property and establish a park, refraining from making such a request to the federal government because they did not want to injure the prospects of the bill pending in Congress to buy the Calaveras groves for a national park.

In 1901, Hill and the Sempervirens Club found sponsors for a bill in the state legislature, and Hill went to Sacramento for several weeks of lobbying to help get the measure through. Perhaps the strongest argument for preservation of the Big Basin redwoods was what Hill carried with him—a portfolio of stunning photographs he had taken on the group's camping expedition the previous spring. After much anxious work by Hill, along with the sage political advice of key supporters, a rewritten version of the land-acquisition bill was passed by the legislature. A reluctant governor signed the measure after hearing testimony at public meetings that confirmed overwhelming popular support for the expenditure. A year later, a commission selected the acreage for this park—2500 acres of old-growth redwoods, plus 1300 acres of cutover land and chapparal. In exchange for $250,000, California got its first state park.

Federal protection for the coast redwoods

Left: The entrance to Big Basin State Park, 1904.

Above: Emblem of the Sempervirens Fund.

Left: Hollow stump and surrounding trees—a familiar scene in old-growth coast redwood forests.

was not far behind. In 1906, Theodore Roosevelt created the Monterey Forest Reserve, south of Big Basin, and in 1908, the President established the most-visited stand of *Sequoia sempervirens,* Muir Woods National Monument. This 503-acre forest near the Pacific, north of San Francisco, had its beginnings not with Roosevelt or Muir, but with William Kent, a Chicago businessman who had moved to Marin County (where Muir Woods is located) in 1871. Kent learned in 1903 that the virgin timber in this narrow canyon was about to be logged, so he and his wife borrowed $45,000 and bought the property. When a water company wanted to dam a creek below the acreage, which would have turned the forest into a lake, Kent donated the property to the federal government.

Unaccustomed to such generosity, the federal officials at first declined to accept or administer the land, but Kent went to John Muir and Theodore Roosevelt for help. These noted conservationists were able to cut through the government red tape, and the forest became a monument. This original designation did not carry any appropriations, however, and again Kent came to the rescue, paying the cost of upkeep for a road into the property until government funds were secured. Subsequently, Kent was elected to Congress and was instrumental in establishing the National Park Service.

William Kent's one request was that the park be named for Muir, to honor the conservationist's achievements in defending and describing nature. Upon learning that the redwood preserve was to be named for him, John Muir said: 'This is the best tree-lover's monument that could be found in all of the forests of the world. You have done me great honor and I am proud of it. . . . Saving these woods from the axe and saw, from the money changers and water changers (dam builders) is in many ways the most notable service to God and man I have heard of since my forest wanderings began.'

The coast redwoods in the northern part of the state, though sheltering the largest trees of

Opposite: Andrew Hill's photograph of Berry Creek Falls in Big Basin State Park.

Above: William Kent, who purchased the land for Muir Woods and donated it to the federal government. Kent's only request was that this National Monument be named for John Muir.

Left: The main trail of the heavily visited Muir Woods.

their kind, were slower to gain protection. Humboldt and Del Norte counties were logging country, and sentiment there was less easily garnered for setting aside these valuable timber trees. As of 1918, not a single redwood in either county was owned by the state. Some early efforts had been made, including an 1852 resolution introduced in the state legislature to request that the United States Congress set aside all redwood lands. The resolution did not pass.

The serious—and successful—campaigns to save large virgin groves in the lush coastal region began with formation of the Save-the-Redwoods League in 1918. This organization was founded by three naturalists who drove up the new Redwood Highway in 1917 to see the immense forests; they were Dr. John C Merriam, of the University of California; Dr. Fairfield Osborn, president of the American Museum of Natural History; and Madison Grant, chairman of the New York Zoological Society. The visitors were appalled at the devastation left by loggers in these forests, and they exposed those conditions in an article in *National Geographic* magazine. The men also recommended to the director of the National Park Service that a national redwood park be created immediately.

Two proposals for such a park did reach Congress, but both were defeated in the Senate. Concurrently with this legislative effort, Merriam, Osborn and Grant founded the League, for the purpose of buying up choice redwood acreage and donating it as parks. Public response was immediate, and a 1921 state law aided the conservationists by pledging that state funds would match all charitable donations for parklands. Other state measures passed in the 1920s established a regular land-acquisition program for state parks, and the League's careful husbanding of cooperation from timber companies made possible a state park system that now includes 31 redwood parks in northern California.

The Save-the-Redwoods League continues to seek donations and to purchase redwood acreage for addition to parklands. Since 1918 the League has raised more than $31 million and, with matching state funds, purchased 142,000 acres of redwood forest for the public. The league is now concentrating on acquiring watershed properties bordering on redwood parks to further protect the fragile ecology of these ancient forests, for erosion of hillsides and carrying of logging debris into streams bordering the virgin forests threatens to damage or destroy these shallow-rooted trees.

Many other conservationists besides those in the league have recognized the need to extend protection beyond the boundaries of the groves of virgin trees. Since the turn of the century, numerous groups and individuals have proposed a national redwood park that would encompass far greater areas than the collection of relatively small state enclaves could manage. Appropriately, the drive to establish this national park has been led by John Muir's Sierra Club, and the 80-year effort has finally resulted in a park of truly magnificent proportions.

Although significant stands of virgin coast redwoods and surrounding terrain are now protected within park boundaries, citizens and conservation groups fought a battle that was long and costly—in dollars and jobs—and that revealed the worst qualities of government bureaucracies in the process. The setting aside of 106,000 acres in Redwood National Park represents a major achievement, accomplished in large part by the vigilance of Sierra Club members, lawyers and lobbyists, and it is a good example of the clash of interest groups, with an often helpless government caught in the middle.

This classic contemporary struggle began in 1966, when public opinion and congressional sentiment were highly in favor of setting aside large tracts of *Sequoia sempervirens* for a national park. An extensive study of possible park sites, made by the National Park Service with funds from the National Geographic Society, had proposed three alternative park areas, all centering on the Redwood Creek watershed, about 50 miles north of Eureka, where the world's tallest tree is located. The largest of these plans

Above: Emblem of the Save-the-Redwoods League.

Left: Extensive clearcut and erosion at the edge of Redwood National Park. Cutting was done right up to the park boundary.

Opposite: Sunset in Redwood National Park.

encompassed 53,000 acres, substantially less than the Sierra Club's subsequent proposal for a 90,000-acre park (which would still have been one of the nation's smallest federal parks). The Sierra Club proposal became the basis for a joint House-Senate bill, cosponsored by more than 50 members of Congress.

During subcommittee hearings on this bill, the director of the National Park Service and his boss, the Undersecretary of the Interior, testified against any park site along Redwood Creek and in favor of a smaller park in the area of Mill Creek, a site that would add only 7500 acres of virgin trees to parklands and would include much of the state redwood lands already preserved. This government position was a complete about-face from the Park Service's earlier recommendations, and both conservationists and the sponsoring congressmen concluded that the abrupt shift in official thinking resulted from two sources: pressure exerted by logging interests, who wanted to cut the valuable timber along Redwood Creek, and a desire to save money that would have to be spent to purchase these private lands for the larger park proposed in the current bill. The Secretary of the Interior acknowledged as much with the comment, 'We wanted to pick a park, not a fight.'

The department's strategy backfired, though. In 1968 Congress passed and President Johnson signed a park bill that preserved lands along Redwood Creek, rejecting the Mill Creek site. The bill provided a total of $92 million to acquire private lands and protect this treasured natural resource. Yet this legislation was a severe compromise, for it set aside only 58,000 acres of prime lands and provided no buffer zones in the creek basin. The new park comprises a narrow strip of land along the Pacific Coast north of Eureka; it encloses three state parks, which continue to be operated by California authorities.

The logging companies that gave up some lands for the new park still held the heavily forested slopes on all sides of the protected forests, and they kept cutting timber without much supervision or restraint. As the loggers moved into unprotected lands to work, the timber firms began negotiations for their millions of dollars in compensation, and the Sierra Club continued to press for its original proposal for a much larger park.

For a few years no major changes were made in the economy of the region, the regulation of logging activities, or the acquisition of land to be added to the park. From the time of the passage of the park bill, however, Sierra Club spokespersons had urged the Interior Department to use its authority under the new law to protect the vital watershed of Redwood Creek by enlarging the boundaries of the protected lands and seeking cooperative agreements with timber

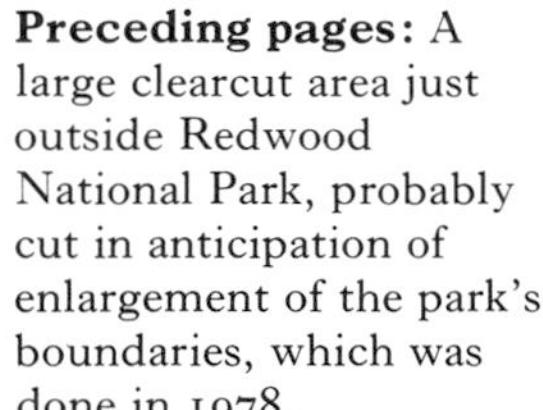

Preceding pages: A large clearcut area just outside Redwood National Park, probably cut in anticipation of enlargement of the park's boundaries, which was done in 1978.

Below: Aerial view of the Tall Tree Grove on Redwood Creek in Redwood National Park, which contains the tallest known coast redwood, 368 feet high.

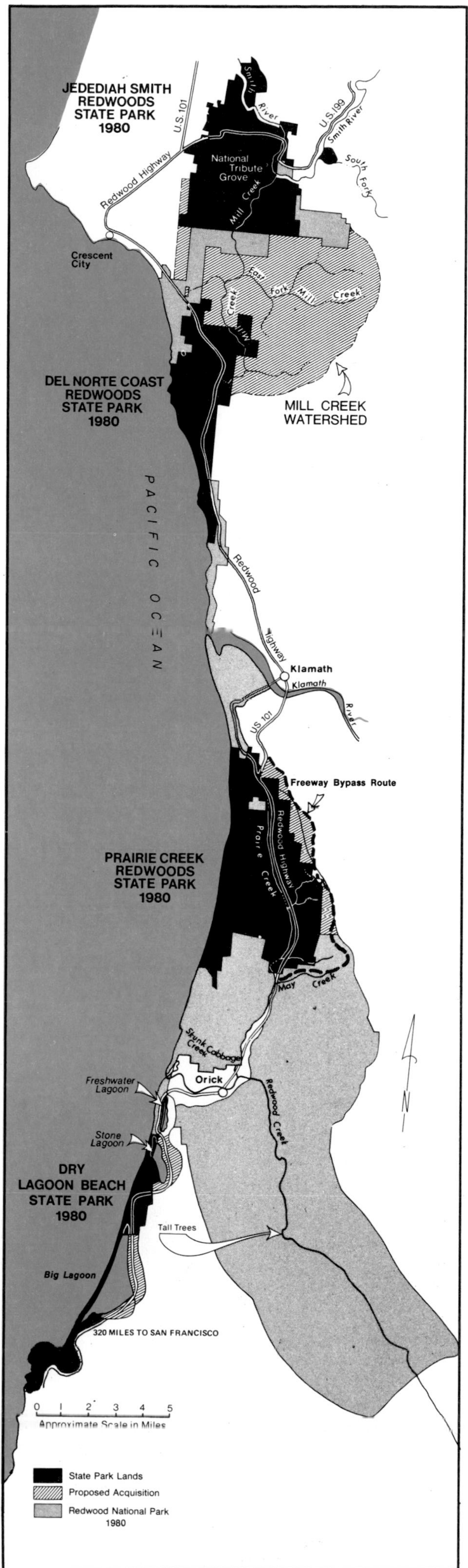

companies regarding their cutting of forests bordering the park.

In 1972 the Interior Department appointed a task force to study the Redwood National Park situation—to update the master plan for the park and to assess the condition of the Redwood Creek watershed in light of the continued logging nearby. The Sierra Club requested a copy of this report but was not given one, so its legal division sued for release of the study under the Freedom of Information Act. In 1973 a court ruled in favor of the conservation group, and the report was released. Its findings confirmed what Sierra Club and other observers had predicted: extensive logging in the watershed areas outside park boundaries had caused massive erosion and buildups of silt, gravel and debris in the streams draining into Redwood Creek and its smaller tributaries within the park. The continued erosion and debris-swollen streams threatened to undermine the shallow roots of the huge trees, and the chances of flood damage increased with every rainstorm. Protection of the virgin stands of *Sequoia sempervirens* that had been set aside in 1968 could not be assured unless immediate controls were placed on logging outside the park.

Specifically, this report recommended that no logging be permitted in areas prone to landslide (which includes much of the watershed), that no logging be done for two years within 75

feet of tributary streams that feed directly into parklands, and that the government purchase an 800-foot buffer zone around these critical streams, which would cost an estimated $15 to $16 million. The federal budget office would not approve any such expenditure, or even permit mention of it in the subsequent publicly released version of the study.

The Interior Department and its National Park Service responded to this report by authorizing another study in 1973, this one to include geologic data prepared by Richard Janda of the US Geological Survey. The NPS also began a new round of talks with the three timber companies operating on the park's borders—Arcata National Corporation, Simpson Timber Company and Louisiana-Pacific Corporation—in hopes of encouraging them to limit voluntarily some of their cutting. The agency took no other action on the first report's recommendations, however.

Left: Map showing California state parklands, Redwood National Park and further acquisitions for parklands proposed by the Save-the-Redwoods League in Del Norte and Humboldt counties, California, 1980.

By 1974 the situation had not changed—all three timber companies were cutting within the area that would have been the 800-foot buffer zone had the Park Service taken its own advice. Erosion damage was becoming more apparent inside the park, and two northern California legislators—congressmen and brothers Phillip and John Burton—introduced a bill to enlarge the park to 132,000 acres. This bill was buried in committee, and in 1975 Phil Burton again introduced the measure, pointing out that more than 10,000 acres of land adjoining the park had been logged since 1968 and that massive erosion had resulted, even threatening the precious grove along Redwood Creek that contains the world's tallest tree. Burton criticized the Interior Department for 'a pattern of indifference, indecisiveness, and frustration' and suggested that only Congress could move to save the invaluable lands that had already been set aside by preserving all of the adjacent watershed.

Also in 1975, the Sierra Club sued Secretary of the Interior Rogers Morton for failure to enforce the law that had established the original park. The suit argued that at least two internal studies prepared by Park Service experts had found damage and had prescribed methods of alleviating that damage, but that the secretary and his subordinates had ignored these recommendations and knowingly allowed the deterioration of the parklands to continue. One witness supporting the Sierra Club's contentions was Janda, the geologist who had prepared the second study for the Park Service; he testified that the situation was already so grave that his research might well be a post mortem for the world's tallest trees rather than a means of saving them. The federal judge hearing this case ruled in favor of the Sierra Club, stating that the 'Department of the Interior has unreasonably and arbitrarily refused and neglected' its responsibility under the law, and he ordered the secretary to prepare a 'reasonable' plan of action within five months.

The report filed by the Interior Department in response to the judge's order claimed that the agency had no further power to act—in purchasing property as a buffer zone or in repairing any damage within the park—because all the original $92 million in appropriations for the park had been spent, and timber companies were suing for higher compensation awards as well. The secretary passed the buck to the President, the only person with power under this law to provide more funds for park protection. At this point, the Sierra Club filed a contempt of court suit, contending that the Interior Secretary had not prepared any plan of action. Early in 1976, the same judge who had earlier ruled for the conservation group this time dismissed the latter suit, agreeing that the government agency's hands were tied by lack of funds.

By this time the Redwood Creek watershed was becoming a *cause célèbre* for loggers and conservationists. The uncut land bordering the southern part of the creek had come to be known as 'the worm,' for it was a winding green swath of parkland between thousands of acres of denuded hills that had been clearcut by logging companies. One report by Park Service surveyors detailed the devastation to 'the worm': 'The upper 10 miles of Redwood Creek is choked with logging debris, collapsed bridges and sediment. In the remainder of the stream alluvial deposits up to 30 feet deep were observed. All but 5 percent of the original stream bank is buried by eroded sediment. About 60 percent of the adjacent slopes are unstable or sliding. Approximately 80 percent of the immediate watershed has been logged in a manner detrimental to the stream.'

The logging companies asserted their right to harvest the timber on their lands, and they produced reports claiming that clearcutting (removing all trees and other plant life from a designated area, usually with the aid of heavy machinery) of timber allows new trees to sprout quickly. The manager of Simpson Timber Company defended his firm's logging practices by noting that 'if you cut down only half the trees, it means you tear up the soil once and then come back in five years to tear it up again

Right: Aerial view of 'the worm' of old-growth redwoods along Redwood Creek, at center. New growth in cutover areas can be seen on either side of the narrow band of remaining large trees.

when you get the other half. With clearcutting you get it all at once, and leave it alone for 50 years.' Other loggers maintained that the erosion was caused more by natural conditions than by the sudden removal of all the trees from steep hillsides, but too much evidence to the contrary limited the credibility of that argument. For example, another Park Service study showed that a stream where loggers had taken only 32 percent of the timber along its banks contained 10 times the turbidity and sedimentation found in a comparable stream where no logging had been done.

The mounting evidence of immediate danger to the park's virgin trees and the continued refusal of the three timber companies to refrain from clearcutting in the Redwood Creek watershed became a nationwide issue in 1977. By this time the state of California had made stricter regulations governing all logging practices, and both President Carter and the new Interior Secretary, Cecil Andrus, had asked the timber firms to accept a voluntary moratorium on cutting trees on land under consideration in the latest park expansion bill, introduced by Phil Burton and California Senator Alan Cranston. One firm, Arcata, defied the request by beginning to cut along a major stream, Skunk Cabbage Creek, on the first day of logging season in 1977. This action led to a rather unprecedented seizure of 35 acres of land along the creek by Secretary Andrus, who was acting with legal sanction of the original park bill and using money donated by the Save-the-Redwoods League.

This action may have turned the tide toward expansion of the park in the minds of members of Congress and the public. Even the hometown newspaper of the redwood logging region, the Eureka *Times-Standard,* editorialized against the Arcata logging move. 'If there was one area of private land surrounding the Redwood National Park which was guaranteed to spark action, immediate action, by conservation groups and the federal government, it was the Skunk Cabbage Creek area. . . . The Secretary of the Interior was not only empowered but obligated to acquire additional lands, on a small scale, both for viewshed protection and protection of the existing park. . . . Cecil Andrus, in taking the 35 acres . . . was acting legally. And we have no doubt—cynical though we are—that he was forced into that exact action by the timber company.'

The loggers themselves, however, bitterly protested any expansion of Redwood National Park, and they demonstrated their point of view loud and clear. Signs and bumper stickers appeared in the north coast region, with such slogans as 'Sierra Club—Kiss My Axe.' When Congressman Phil Burton held hearings in Eureka and San Francisco in connection with

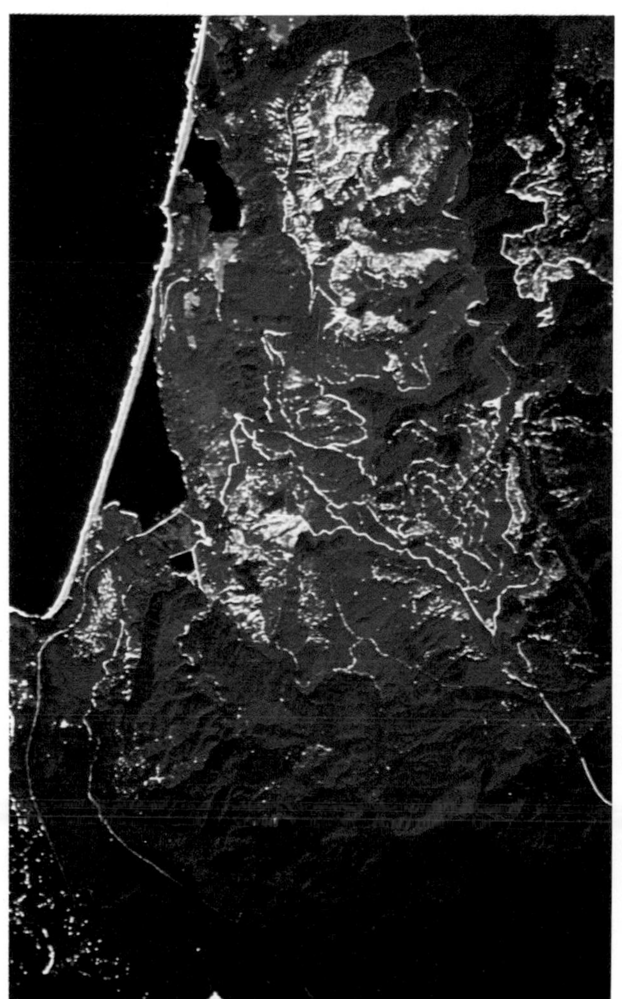

Far left: Infrared view of the three lagoons just north of Eureka. The dark red areas are virgin redwood forest; the lighter red areas nearer the coast are second growth after logging; and the white areas are the recently cutover lands and logging roads.

Left: The enormous wooden statue of a lumberjack, a tourist attraction on the edge of Redwood National Park; note the people seated on his foot.

his expansion bill, the loggers packed the hearing rooms and made an unsuccessful attempt to tie up traffic on the Golden Gate Bridge with their logging trucks to gain public attention for their cause. A month later, in May 1977, a convoy of logging trucks drove across the country to demonstrate outside the nation's capitol, again protesting the loss of jobs and tax base that park enlargement would mean. One of these trucks carried a huge redwood log carved in the shape of a peanut—the loggers' crude message to President Carter, who supported expansion of the national park.

One state report estimated that 2200 jobs would be lost in the region if major park expansion took place, although the manager of the state unemployment office in Eureka disputed that claim, noting that only a few hundred jobs would be lost. Moreover, the 1977 version of the park expansion bill contained a provision for $40 million in aid to all logging-related workers who lost employment because of lands taken out of timber production. When this additional section was added to the legislation, much of the loggers' protest against it lost urgency.

The timber firms pressed their case against park expansion through lobbying efforts in Washington, DC. Their chief spokesman was James G O'Hara, a former congressman who had cosponsored the original Sierra Club-backed bill for a 90,000-acre park in 1967. O'Hara worked with a Washington law firm that registered as lobbyists for the Redwood Industry Park Committee in June of 1977. Known as a parliamentarian and shrewd political thinker, O'Hara hoped to lead a last-minute derailing of the legislation to add substantial acreage (48,000 acres in one sponsor's bill, 74,000 in

Opposite: The junction of Goodwood Creek and Miner's Ridge trails in Prairie Creek Redwoods State Park.

Right: This old logger's axe buried in a redwood stump near the national park is a symbol of many lumber workers' and loggers' feelings about the likely effect of expanded parklands on their industry.

Below: The caravan of logging trucks traveling to Washington, DC, to protest against expansion of Redwood National Park in May, 1977. The lead truck carries a huge redwood log cut in the shape of a peanut as a message to then-President Carter. The loggers called this their 'Talk to America' convoy.

another) to the park. His and other opponents' attempts failed, though, and the two houses of Congress passed separate versions of the bill, which were reconciled in a conference committee in March 1978. The votes were 328–60 in the House and 74–20 in the Senate. President Carter signed the bill on March 27, 1978.

The expansion of Redwood National Park added 48,000 acres to the protected lands, providing $359 million for acquisition of these lands and for rehabilitation of areas that suffered the effects of clearcutting and erosion. A second provision of the new law provided $40 million to compensate workers who lose their jobs or sustain reductions in income because of park enlargement; these funds also cover retraining of workers for new vocations or moving expenses if they choose to leave the area and work elsewhere.

Despite the job-loss compensation provisions in the new law—which are unique to this park legislation—people in the logging region were angry at their defeat. When the bill passed, the mayor of Eureka noted, 'We were living in a fool's paradise. We thought Washington worked like a democracy. What you've really got is government by arm-twisting.' One sawmill workers union official was less hard on the government, conceding that 'as much as we fought Phil Burton on this thing, we also have to give him credit. He said he would help the workers, and he has.'

Other residents of the logging region are distrustful of both the compensation promises and the intentions of environmentalists, predicting that another 'land grab' could begin at any time. The president of Arcata's timber division stated, 'Personally, I don't think [the environmentalists] will ever stop. I believe they will keep coming back until they have everything so tied up no one will be able to continue operating.'

The Sierra Club's president refuted that suspicion, stating, 'We now have the essentials for the magnificent park that we wanted. It will not be an instant park; it may, in fact, take

1▲

◄2

3▲

4▼

(1) The impressive entrance to Arcata Redwood Company. (2) The coastline immediately north of Point Delgada in Humboldt County, one of the few coastal wilderness areas left in California. (3) The spectacular coastal enclave of Georgia-Pacific Lumber Company at Fort Bragg. (4) A plant in Eureka that manufactures redwood burl products, now a growing industry in this region.

decades to grow into the park it will become one day. And there still may be problems with erosion from upstream. But I don't expect we will have to go back to Congress again. I hope it is over.'

The major battle does seem to be over, but there has been fallout on both sides. The timber companies have cut virgin timber that would have been included in a park had they accepted the requested moratorium, and they have filed compensation claims for appropriated parklands that far exceed the amount Congress allocated for this purpose. In late 1978, the federal government had paid Arcata $60.3 million for 11,000 acres purchased in the 1978 park expansion, and that firm continues to press for an additional $20 to $40 million in compensation for the land. Louisiana-Pacific, which lost 27,000 acres to the 1978 expansion, has received $128.6 million in partial payment and is disputing the maximum value of $230 million placed on this land by the government.

Some observers, including the late Congressman Leo Ryan of northern California, noted that timber company claims were unreasonably high and that the abrupt rise in redwood lumber prices just as the government began assessing the value of new parklands was possibly the result of price-fixing (particularly because the three timber firms whose land was purchased for the park are the prime holders of remaining old-growth redwoods). The timber firms denied this allegation, however, and the charge has not been substantiated.

Some of the loggers and lumbermill workers of the Eureka area (the site of major sawmills since redwood cutting began in the 1850s) have lost their jobs, but the number put out of work by the park is in the hundreds, not the thousands predicted by some industry sources. Louisiana-Pacific closed a plywood-making plant in the area as a result of its loss of redwood acreage to the park, and 265 workers were laid off by that action. These workers are being compensated by the special provisions and funds in the park expansion bill, although the wheels of government indeed grind slowly—especially for out-of-work people. One mill worker who was laid off had to wait 10 months to receive the first payment from the compensation program, and she had to file additional claims and wait several more months for medical benefits also promised in the bill.

Below Left: A perfect specimen of redwood burl, with its characteristic rich patterning of fine grain.

Below: A National Park Service diagram showing the stages of reclamation of eroded and cutover areas.

All these benefits were late because the federal government, in its laborious wisdom, passed the funding appropriation for worker compensation six months after the President signed the park bill into law. Thus, the layoffs came long before the payments to workers, although once started, these benefits could continue for up to six years for workers who had been employed in the timber industry for five years or more before losing their jobs. Unlike the relatively small stipend provided by state unemployment insurance (which these workers used until the federal government got its program under way), the park compensation bill allows payment at the full salary or hourly wage of the affected workers.

Although hundreds of thousands of *Sequoia sempervirens* were saved permanently by the two-stage creation of Redwood National Park, a few old trees were destroyed by chainsaw-wielding vandals during the height of tension over the park's enlargement in 1978. Ten virgin trees in state park reserves were killed and eight more were severely damaged in the senseless action, which brought charges from both environmentalists and loggers that their opponents had taken this vicious action to gain publicity for their cause. State park rangers began additional patrols of the parkland and several timber industry groups offered rewards for the arrest of the vandals, but no culprit was ever

Opposite: A restful creekside scene of virgin redwoods and alders.

Left: Sign showing current use fees for a California State Park in the redwood region.

Below: Small-scale horse logging in Humboldt County. An industry of independent loggers who do not use machines in the forest has developed among people who wish to have a minimum impact on the woodland environment.

found. One local sheriff's investigator expressed the prevailing sentiment regarding the person responsible for harming the redwoods: 'I hope a tree falls on this guy.'

Violence to the redwood trees is a rare and plainly regrettable action by someone disturbed beyond control. Fortunately, it is not typical of the attitude of even the most outspoken opponents of preservation of large tracts of redwoods; rather, the men and women who cut the trees and work the timber are often among the most reverent forest dwellers. Today some of these timber people are working alongside preservation-minded citizens at new jobs created by the redwood park—rehabilitating the watershed that was damaged by the decade of logging before a slow-moving government preserved its forests for good. If these foresters and the still-active timber companies continue to exercise good timber-management practices and judicious harvesting techniques, both the redwood parklands and the redwood tree farms should provide their resources—magnificent standing groves and usable lumber products—for centuries to come.

Below left: An early expedition into the Big Basin forest at the turn of the century; the campers are probably members of the Sempervirens Club.

. . . the greatest beauty is organic wholeness,
the wholeness of life and things,
the divine beauty of the universe. Love that,
not man apart from that . . .
—ROBINSON JEFFERS

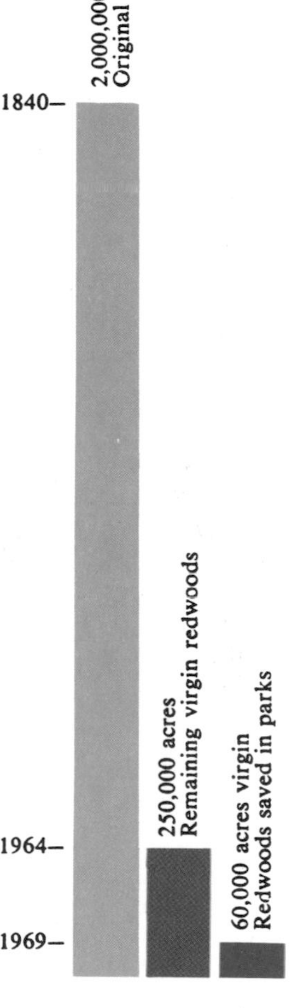

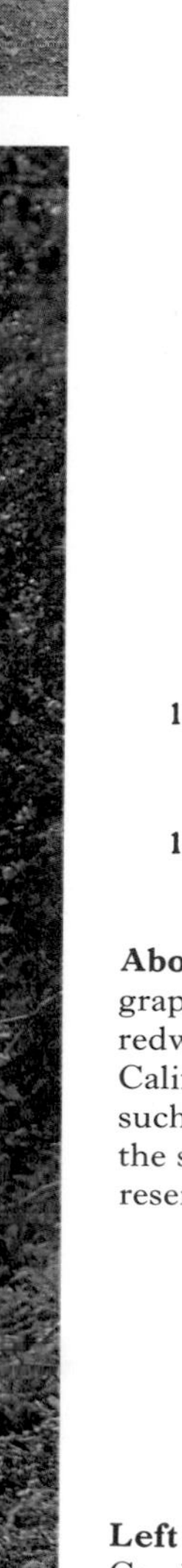

Above: A Sierra Club graph showing virgin redwoods originally in California, the acreage of such trees remaining in the state and the acreage reserved in parklands.

Left: Hikers in Prairie Creek Redwoods State Park.

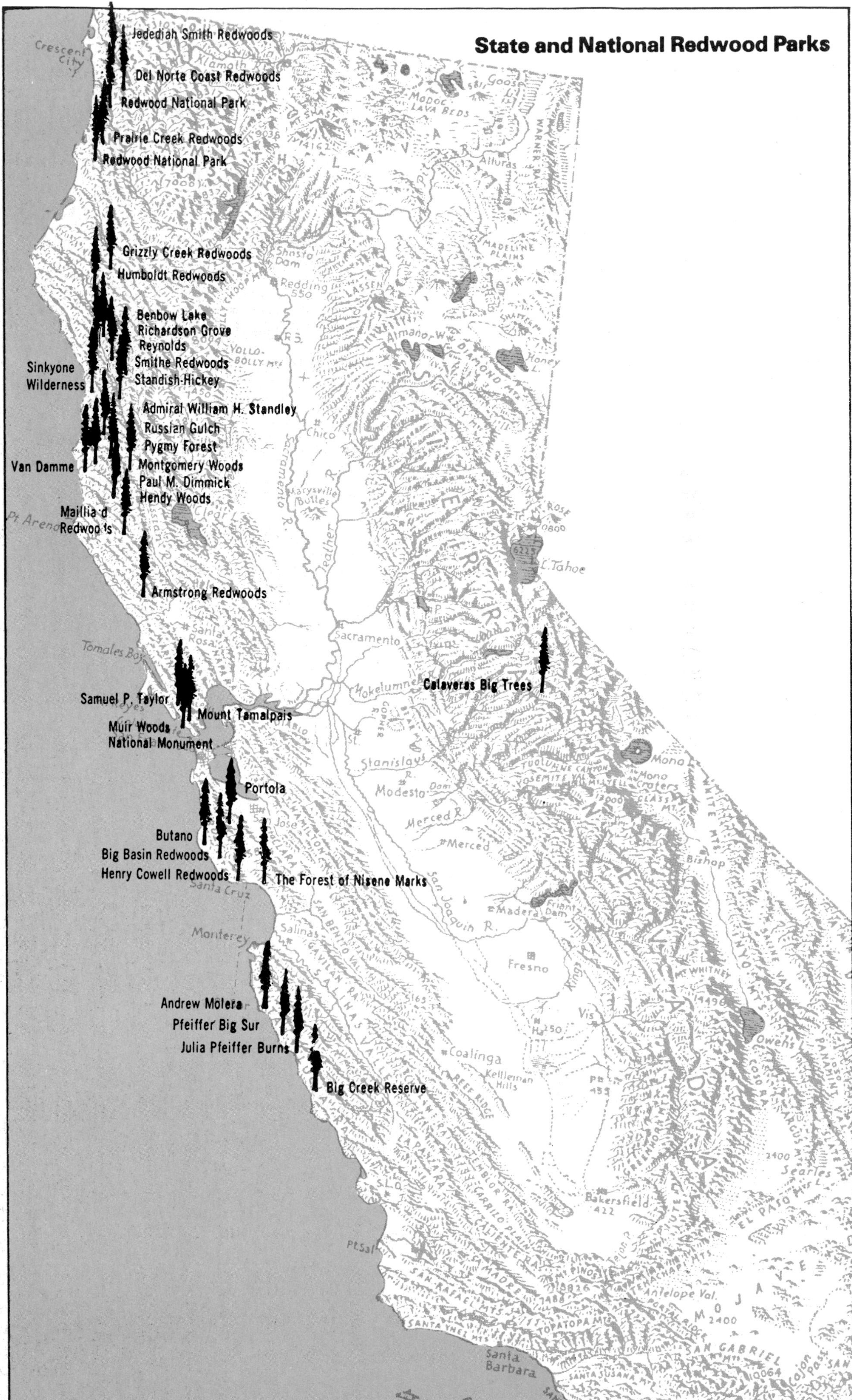

Right: The state and national parklands protecting sequoias in California, 1980.

Opposite: A one-man sawmill operation near Occidental, in Sonoma County. Such small operations have become viable as redwood has become scarce and timber's value has increased in recent years.

Following pages: Hale Tharp's cabin at the edge of Log Meadow in the Giant Forest of Sequoia National Park. Tharp discovered and protected this magnificent grove of Big Trees.

RICO CALVI — SAWMILL OCCIDENTAL, CALIFORNIA Art Rogers 1980

TOM KENT — TREE SERVICE INVERNESS PARK, CALIFORNIA Art Rogers 1975

Opposite: An independent logger with the latest equipment and his latest conquest.

Above: Rangers of the Point Reyes National Seashore, in Marin County, assembled in a redwood grove in the park.

THE EXAMPLE OF BULL CREEK

THE IMPORTANCE OF BOTH ADEQUATE WATERSHED protection and good forest maintenance became painfully clear at Bull Creek (near Garberville in Humboldt County, California), in a stand of trees purchased in 1931 by the Save-the-Redwoods League. Named Rockefeller Forest for the major contribution to its purchase by John D Rockefeller, Jr., this old-growth area consists of 9400 acres in a flat stand of some of the tallest redwoods anywhere. Bull Creek runs through this mighty forest, flowing down a watershed that measures 41 square miles and covers 26,000 acres, from elevations of 3400 feet at the highest ridge to 130 feet at the creek bottom. Ground-level marks on the trees show that floods had occurred here about every 50 years since the year 1000, but the virgin forest had not been dislodged or greatly disturbed by any of these events.

In 1947, however, hit-and-run loggers began stripping the Bull Creek basin upstream from the protected parkland. They denuded steep hillsides, cut skid tracks and roads into the bare soil and abandoned mountains of debris. The delicate ecological balance that had held for at least 10 centuries in that watershed began to crumble immediately, muddying the streams and driving out the salmon and steelhead that previously had spawned in Bull Creek. By 1954 logging had crippled more than half of this watershed, and fires had burned another 7000 acres.

The manmade stage was set for a catastrophe that nature could have handled if its soils and hillsides had been held in place by the roots of redwood and fir of the upstream forest. Those roots were gone, however, or were so small and far apart that they could not hold, and the rains of December 1955 brought down the watershed. Soil, rocks and debris washed into the creek and its tributaries, causing it to swell into a torrent that plunged through Rockefeller Forest. Within a few hours, 300 major trees (at least 4 feet in diameter) were toppled by the flood, and fully 50 acres of soil were carried away from the forest floor. A logjam 40 feet high formed at one place in the creek, forcing more water and debris out of the banks and increasing the damage—another 99 trees were so badly cut and scarred that they had to be taken down during the cleanup.

A similar flood destroyed 400 more large trees in 1964, and the gentler rains of the winters in between brought more damage to this

Opposite: An example of the cutting on slopes that causes massive erosion and damage to watersheds.

Below: Forest fires in logging regions also damage watersheds and destroy trees that would otherwise be available for timber. Like cutover areas, burned areas are likely sites for erosion.

ravaged watershed and forest. Since the second major flood, the state has instituted a program of reclamation, deepening the channel of Bull Creek and lining the banks with rock to prevent further undercutting of the redwoods' shallow roots. Concurrently, the Save-the-Redwoods League has purchased much of the watershed, which was far less valuable after it had been logged and subsequently flooded. All these measures have resulted in the beginnings of recovery for Bull Creek and its basin, but the 800 lost trees are evidence of what human caprice can do to an ancient forest.

The tragic example of Bull Creek offered a lesson to conservationists, and their redoubled efforts have resulted in some public understanding that a forest is more than a grove of trees on a piece of flat ground. Although the politicians seem to have learned much more slowly than the citizens, they too have finally given sanctuary to the greatest of living things. A noted chronicler of trees, Donald Culross Peattie, has spoken a

Right: A clearcut area and the mess left by loggers on Bull Creek.

Right: An effort to prevent flood or erosion damage by widening and deepening the stream channel.

fitting tribute to all the people who made this sanctuary possible:

'It is moving, as one travels through the flickering light and shade of the Redwood Highway, to realize that many of these groves were given, in part at least, by people who have never seen the redwoods and perhaps do not expect ever to see them. For the members of some of the sponsoring organizations live in Iowa or Vermont, in Georgia or New York. The great majority of them are probably not persons of wealth at all. They gave anonymously, they gave purely, they gave to the future, to people yet unborn; they gave not only to the country but to the world. And they gave out of a deep religious feeling that the beauty and age and greatness that here have risen from the earth to tower above us are holy and shall not be profaned.'

Left: A portion of Rockefeller Forest on Bull Creek.

Below: Terracing on the banks of Bull Creek after the disastrous flooding, a concerted effort to save the remaining virgin trees in this prime flat stand.

GLOSSARY

ALBINO—a plant that lacks chlorophyll.

BOARD FOOT—a standard measurement of lumber equal to a board that is 1 foot long, 1 foot wide and 1 inch thick.

BOLE—the trunk of a tree.

BRISTLECONE PINE—the only living tree that is older than the redwoods; it grows in the White Mountains of California and Nevada.

BURL—a rounded, knoblike growth on a tree trunk, usually characterized by the irregularly patterned grain of its wood.

BUTTRESS—a thickened area of a tree's trunk, usually at the base, that provides added support.

CAMBIUM—the growth layer of a tree's trunk and branches, which is only one cell thick but produces all the new wood cells for the tree.

CHLOROPHYLL—the green substance that is essential to photosynthesis in plants.

CLEARCUT—a timber-harvesting process in which all trees are cut in a given area.

CONIFER—a tree that produces its seeds in cones.

DECIDUOUS—a tree that sheds its leaves seasonally.

EROSION—removal of surface soil by rain and wind.

EVERGREEN—a tree that does not shed its leaves or needles seasonally.

FIRE COLUMN—a pattern of new branches that have sprouted along the burned area of a coast redwood tree damaged by a forest fire.

FLAT STAND—a grouping of old-growth coast redwoods of approximately the same height, located on flat ground.

FOG BELT—an area of the northern California coast where natural conditions create fog and high moisture content, favoring the growth of coast redwoods.

GENUS—a subdivision in the classification of plants, indicated by the first word in the botanical name of a plant.

GOOSEPEN—a hollowed out area in the base of a coast redwood tree.

HARDPAN—tightly packed soil through which water will not penetrate.

HEARTWOOD—the innermost layer of a tree's trunk and branches, which consists of tightly packed dead cells that provide strength for the tree.

Metasequoia—the genus name for the dawn redwood, which is native to China.

PHLOEM—the layer of a tree's trunk and branches that carries food downward from the leaves to the rest of the tree and its roots.

PHOTOSYNTHESIS—the chemical process by which green plants convert sunlight and carbon dioxide into food with oxygen as a byproduct.

RINGS—a series of dark and light concentric markings within a tree's trunk that indicate the annual growth of the tree.

Sequoia—the genus name applied to coast redwood trees; also the popular term for both coast redwoods and Big Trees (giant sequoia).

Sequoiadendron—the genus name of the giant sequoia, popularly called the Big Tree or Sierra redwood.

SEQUOYAH—a Cherokee Indian leader whose name is believed to be the source of the botanical name sequoia.

SIERRA NEVADA—the mountain range in eastern California where giant sequoia trees grow.

SLOPE FOREST—a mixture of trees, including coast redwoods, which grow on uneven terrain.

SNAGTOP—a giant sequoia tree that is damaged or dead at the top.

SPECIES—a subdivision in the classification of plants, indicated by the second word in the botanical name of a plant.

SPIKE-TOP—a coast redwood tree that is dead at the top but healthy below.

TRANSPIRATION—the process by which plants release excess moisture from their leaves into the air.

WATERSHED—all the tributary streams and surrounding land of a major creek or river system.

XYLEM—the layer of a tree's trunk and branches that carries water and soil nutrients upward from the roots to the rest of the tree.

SOURCE NOTES

Tree Life

1. Description of redwoods by Fray Crespi noted in several sources, including J C Shirley, *The Redwoods of Coast and Sierra*, p. 11.
2. The botanical squabble is described by J Hoopes in *The Book of Evergreens*, p. 244.
3. Lindley's tribute to Wellington cited in Hartesveldt et al., *The Giant Sequoia of the Sierra Nevada*, p. 23.
4. Douglas's description of the California coast cited in Hoopes, p. 245.
5. Fritz's study reported in 'Story Told by a Fallen Redwood,' a pamphlet from the Save-the-Redwoods League.

God's Own Flagpoles

1. Hee-li's adventures described at length in A Powers, *Redwood Country*.
2. Redwoods described as 'a titan race' in F Leydet, *The Last Redwoods and the Parkland of Redwood Creek*, p. 53.
3. Description of 'God's own flagpoles' from the unpublished memoirs of Louise Mendelsohn.

Mothers of the Forest

1. Leonard's account of discovering the Big Trees cited in many sources, including Hartesveldt et al., p. 2.
2. Fire's importance to the giant sequoia's long survival cited in Hartesveldt et al., p. 101.
3. The threat of damage by carpenter ants living in giant sequoias cited in Hartesveldt et al., p. 134.

The Dawn's Legacy

1. Silverman's and Chaney's accounts of the China journey are reported in L Florin, *Historic Glimpses of Trees of the West*, pp. 17–24.
2. Propagation and use of metasequoias in China today reported in National Academy of Science, *Plant Studies in the People's Republic of China*, and the Food and Agriculture Organization of the United Nations, *China: Integrated Wood Processing Industries*.

Native American Wilderness

1. *Gleason's Pictorial* comments cited in Hartesveldt et al., p. 6.

Using the Trees

1. The proliferation of giant sequoias in Britain cited in R J Hartesveldt, 'Sequoias in Europe,' unpublished manuscript.
2. Additional documentation of redwoods throughout the world cited in E E Stanford, 'Redwoods Away,' the Eighth Annual College of the Pacific Faculty Research Lecture, 19 May 1958.

Protecting the Trees

1. Theodore Roosevelt's trip to Yosemite with John Muir cited in S Sargent, *John Muir in Yosemite*, p. 35.
2. John Muir's tribute to wilderness parks cited in F Tilden, *The National Parks*, p. 22.
3. John Muir's thanks for the naming of Muir Woods cited in the National Park Service brochure on Muir Woods.
4. Principal documentation of the fight to save the Redwood Creek watershed and enlarge Redwood National Park provided by documents and files of the Sierra Club and the *Sierra Club Bulletin*.
5. Phillip Burton's comments about the need to enlarge Redwood National Park included in mimeographed copy of his introduction of his bill, 11 March 1975.
6. Park Service surveyors' report of logging damage to Redwood Creek watershed cited in R A Jones, 'Officials Question Value of 1973 Reform Program,' Los Angeles *Times*, 24 August 1975.
7. Editorial in Eureka *Times-Standard* appeared 12 June 1977.
8. Comments of workers, logging company officials and Sierra Club president cited in R A Jones, 'Eureka a Victim of the Redwood War,' Los Angeles *Times*, 8 March 1978.
9. Donald Culross Peattie's tribute to all who who helped establish redwood parks cited in Leydet, p. 98.

BIBLIOGRAPHY

ANDREWS, Ralph W. *Redwood Classic*. Seattle: Superior Publishing Company, 1958.

ANTHROP, Donald F. *Redwood State and National Parks*. Happy Camp, CA: Naturegraph Publishers, 1977.

ARNO, Stephen F. *Discovering Sierra Trees*. Yosemite, CA: Yosemite Natural History Association, 1973.

'Attacks on the Redwoods.' Los Angeles *Times*, 27 January 1978.

BAKER, Richard St. Barbe. *The Redwoods*. London: George Ronald, 1943, 1960.

BAKKER, Elna. *An Island Called California*. Berkeley: University of California Press, 1971.

BURTON, Phillip. 'Comments on Introduction of Legislation to Expand the Redwood National Park.' Mimeographed copy, March 1975.

BYTHERIVER, Marylee. *A Citizen's Guide to Timber Harvest Plans*. Covelo, CA: Island Press, 1979.

BYTHERIVER, Marylee. 'Timber 2000—From Where It Stands Today.' *Cry California*, Spring 1980, pp. 19–23.

'California Giants,' *Chambers Journal*, 20 December 1856, pp. 398–99.

CARDWELL, Kenneth H. *Bernard Maybeck: Artisan, Architect, Artist*. Santa Barbara, CA: Peregrine Smith, 1977.

CARRIGHAR, Sally. *One Day on Bettle Rock*. New York: Knopf, 1944.

CAVAGNARO, David. *Audubon Canyon Ranch*. Stinson Beach, CA: Audubon Canyon Ranch, no date.

CHANEY, Ralph W. 'Redwoods of the Past.' San Francisco: Save-the-Redwoods League, 1934, 1977.

China's Integrated Wood Processing Industries. Rome: Food and Agriculture Organization of the United Nations, 1979.

CLARK, Galen. *Big Trees of California*. Yosemite Valley, CA: Galen Clark, 1907.

The CoEvolution Quarterly, published by the *Whole Earth Catalog*. Various issues, including 'Treelife,' Summer 1979.

DAVENPORT, Howard E. *California Big Trees*. Stockton, CA: Calaveras Grove Association, 1949.

DAVIS, Douglas F, and Holderman, Dale F. *The White Redwoods*. Happy Camp, CA: Naturegraph Publishers, 1980.

DE VRIES, Carolyn. *Grand and Ancient Forest: The Story of Andrew P. Hill and Big Basin Redwoods State Park*. Fresno, CA: Valley Publishers, 1978.

DOYLE, Bill. 'Eying the Economy.' Oakland *Tribune*, 22 September 1976.

DURRENBERGER·JOHNSON. *California, Patterns on the Land*. Palo Alto, CA: Mayfield Publishing Company, 1976.

ENGBECK, Joseph H, Jr. *The Enduring Giants*. Berkeley: University of California Press, 1973.

FARB, Peter, and the Editors of *Life*. *The Forest*. New York: Time, Inc., 1961.

FARQUHAR, Francis P. *History of the Sierra Nevada*. Berkeley: University of California Press, 1965.

FLORIN, Lambert. *Historic Glimpses of Trees of the West*. Seattle: Superior Publishing Company, 1977.

FOGARTY, John. 'House OKs Expansion of the Redwood Park.' San Francisco *Chronicle*, 10 February 1978.

FOWLES, John. 'Seeing Nature Whole.' *Harper's*, November 1979, pp. 49–68.

FRITZ, Emanuel. 'Story Told by a Fallen Red-Redwood.' San Francisco: Save-the-Redwoods League, 1934, 1978.

GOLDSMITH, Edward. 'A Man of the Trees: Interview with Dr. Richard St. Barbe Baker.' *The Ecologist*, October–November 1979, reprinted in *CoEvolution Quarterly*, Spring 1980, pp. 66–69.

'Grab Bag.' San Francisco *Chronicle*, 16 August 1980.

GRAY, A A; Farquhar, F P; and Lewis, W S. *Camels in Western America*. San Francisco: California Historical Society, 1930.

HARTESVELDT, R J. 'Sequoias in Europe.' Unpublished manuscript in the Forestry School Library of the University of California at Berkeley, 1969.

HARTESVELDT, Richard J; Harvey, H Thomas; Shellhammer, Howard; and Stecker, Ronald. *The Giant Sequoia of the Sierra Nevada*. Washington, D.C.: US Department of the Interior, National Park Service, 1975.

HERSCHLER, J Barton. *Muir Woods National Monument* (Rev. ed.). San Rafael, CA: Muir Woods-Point Reyes Association, 1968.

HOOPES, Josiah. *The Book of Evergreens*. New York: Orange Judd & Company, 1868.

HUME, Ellen. 'Investigation of Redwood Prices Asked.' Los Angeles *Times*, 9 August 1978.

HUTCHINGS, J M. *The Mammoth Trees of Calaveras* (1872). Olympic Valley, CA: Outbooks, 1978.

'Innumerable Uses of Redwood.' *Architect & Engineer*, March 1940, pp. 21 ff.

JEPSON, Willis Linn. *The Trees of California* (2nd ed.). Berkeley: Associated Students Store, 1923.

JEPSON, Willis Linn. 'Trees, Shrubs and Flowers of the Redwood Region.' San Francisco: Save-the-Redwoods League, 1934, 1976.

JOHNSON, David. 'Shock in Redwood Country.' Los Angeles *Times*, 26 January 1978.

JOHNSON, Hugh. *The International Book of Trees*. London: Mitchell Beazley Publishers, 1973.

JOHNSTON, Hank. *They Felled the Redwoods*. Los Angeles: Trans-Anglo Books, 1966.

JONES, Robert A. 'Eureka a Victim of the Redwood War.' Los Angeles *Times*, 8 March 1978.

JONES, Robert A. 'Logging Damage to Redwood Park Cited.' Los Angeles *Times*, 9 November 1975.

JONES, Robert A. 'Officials Question Value of 1973 Reform Program.' Los Angeles *Times*, 24 August 1975.

JONES, Robert A. 'Younger Asks Halt to Logging Near Park.' Los Angeles *Times*, 18 November 1975.

'Just Who Are Area's Friends?' (editorial). Eureka *Times-Standard*, 12 June 1977.

KETCHUM, Richard M. *The Secret Life of the Forest*. New York; American Heritage Press, 1970.

KROEBER, A L. *Handbook of the Indians of California*. New York: Dover, 1976.

LANDON, Joan. 'Blacklist Confiscated from Mills.' Eureka *Times-Standard*, 5 May 1977.

LANE, Ferdinand C. *The Story of Trees*. Garden City, NY: Doubleday, 1953.

'Legislators Argue that Redwood Creek Is the Best Site for a National Park.' *Sierra Club Bulletin*, August 1967, pp. 5–20.

LEYDET, Francois. *The Last Redwoods and the Parkland of Redwood Creek*. San Francisco: Sierra Club·Ballantine Books, 1969.

LIBBEY, Mike. 'Loggers Blitz SF Hearing.' Oakland *Tribune*, 14 April 1977.

LINDSAY, A D, and Lane-Poole, C E. 'California Big Trees.' Commonwealth Forestry, leaflet No. 13, Australia, 1932.

'Loggers Head for Washington.' San Francisco *Chronicle*, 16 May 1977.

'Loggers Take Park Protest to Congress.' *AFL-CIO News*, 4 June 1977.

MARGOLIN, Malcolm. *The East Bay Out*. Berkeley: Heyday Books, 1974.

MATTHEWES, William H, III. *A Guide to the National Parks*. Garden City, NY: Doubleday· Natural History Press, 1973.

MCCORMICK, Jack. *The Life of the Forest*. New York: McGraw-Hill, 1966.

'Menaced Redwoods.' Norfolk *Virginian-Pilot*, 23 May 1977.

MERRIAM, John C. 'A Living Link in History.' San Francisco: Save-the-Redwoods League, 1934, 1978.

MORLEY, Jim. *Muir Woods*. Berkeley: Howell-North Books, 1968.

MOSS, Larry E. 'The New Redwood National Park.' *Sierra Club Bulletin*, January-February 1979 (unpaged reprint).

MUIR, John. *The Coniferous Forests and Big Trees of the Sierra Nevada* (1881). Olympic Valley, CA: Outbooks, 1977.

MUIR, John. *The Proposed Yosemite National Park —Treasures and Features* (1890). Olympic Valley, CA: Outbooks, 1976.

MUIR, John. *A Rival of the Yosemite: The Canyon of the South Fork of King's River, California* (1891). Olympic Valley, CA: 1978.

NATIONAL ACADEMY OF SCIENCES. *Plant Studies in the People's Republic of China*. Washington, D.C.: National Academy of Science, 1975.

NATIONAL PARK SERVICE. 'Environmental Assessment: Management Options for the Redwood Creek Corridor, Redwood National Park.' 3 November 1975.

NEW ZEALAND FOREST SERVICE. '50th Anniversary, 1919–1969.' Pamphlet, 1969.

NICHOLS, Nan, 'Loggers Confront Crisis.' Sacramento *Bee*, 28 November 1977.

NIXON, Stuart. *Redwood Empire*. New York: Galahad Books, 1966.

OAKESHOTT, Gordon B. *California's Changing Landscapes*. New York: McGraw-Hill, 1971.

ORNDUFF, Robert. *Introduction to California Plant Life*. Berkeley: University of California Press, 1974.

PLATT, Rutherford. *The Great American Forest*. Engelwood Cliffs, NJ: Prentice-Hall, 1965.

POWERS, Alfred. *Redwood Country*. New York: Duell, Sloan and Pearce, 1949.

'Producing Redwood Lumber.' *Architect & Engineer*, March 1940, pp. 19–20.

'Proposed Expansion of the Redwood National Park: The Industry's View.' Pamphlet distributed by Lumber and Sawmill Workers' unions and Arcata Redwood Company and Louisiana-Pacific Corporation. No date or place of publication.

RAPHAEL, Ray. *An Everyday History of Somewhere*. Covelo, CA: Island Press, 1980 (formerly published by Knopf, out of print).

RAPHAEL, Ray. *Tree Talk: The People and Politics of Timber*. Covelo, CA: Island Press, 1981.

RENNERT, Leo. 'Log Truckers Roll into Washington, Launch Lobby Effort on Redwoods.' Sacramento *Bee*, 24 May 1977.

RENNERT, Leo. (Redwood Park Advocate Switches Jobs, Support.' Sacramento *Bee*, 16 August 1977.

RICHARDSON, Stanley D. *Forestry in Communist China*. Baltimore: Johns Hopkins Press, 1966.

ROBINSON, John, and Calais, Alfred. *California State Parks*. Menlo Park, CA: Lane Books, 1966.

RUBENSTEIN, Steve. 'Tall Trees and Angry Loggers.' San Francisco *Chronicle*, 30 April 1977.

SARGENT, Shirley. *John Muir in Yosemite*. Yosemite, CA: Flying Spur Press, 1971.

'Science News.' US Forest Products Labratory, Madison, Wisconsin, 1967.

SHINOFF, Paul. 'The Loggers Who Lost Their Jobs.' San Francisco *Examiner*, 15 October 1978.

SHIRLEY, James Clifford. *The Redwoods of Coast and Sierra*. Berkeley: University of California Press, 1937.

STANFORD, Ernest E. 'Redwoods Away.' The Eighth Annual College of the Pacific Faculty Research Lecture, 19 May 1958.

STRONG, Douglas Hillman. *Trees—or Timber? The Story of Sequoia and Kings Canyon National Parks*. Three Rivers, CA: Sequoia Natural History Association, 1968.

SMITH, Gladys L. *Flowers and Ferns of Muir Woods*. San Rafael, CA: Muir Woods Natural History Association, 1963.

TAYLOR, Norman. *The Ageless Relicts*. New York: St Martin's Press, 1962.

TEALE, Edwin Way (ed.). *The Wilderness World of John Muir*. Boston: Houghton Mifflin, 1954.

TILDEN, Freeman. *The National Parks* (Rev. ed.). New York: Knopf, 1970.

TODD, John. 'Who Killed the Trees, and Why?' San Francisco *Examiner*, 22 January 1978.

'Two Firms Losing Redwood Timberland to Seek Substantial Compensation Boost.' *Wall Street Journal*, 29 March 1978.

'US Pays 2 Firms for Lands Taken in Park Expansion.' *Wall Street Journal*, 21 September 1978.

WAYBURN, Edgar, and Wayburn, Peggy. 'The Short, Sorry History of Redwood National Park.' *Sierra Club Bulletin*, October 1975; November–December 1973; June 1971 (unpaged reprint).

WEAVER, Harriet E. *Adventures in the Redwoods*. San Francisco: Chronicle Books, 1975.

WESTON, G C. 'The Role of Exotic Genera Other than *Pinus* in New Zealand Forestry.' Forest Research Institute, Rotorua, New Zealand, 1971.

WHITNEY, Stephen. *A Sierra Club Naturalist's Guide to the Sierra Nevada*. San Francisco: Sierra Club Books, 1979.

WILEY, Walt. 'Redwoods Battle Lines Are Drawn.' Sacramento *Bee*, 7 April 1977.

WILKERSON, Hugh, and van der Zee, John. *Life in the Peace Zone*. New York: Collier Books, 1971.

WOOD, Nancy. *Clearcut*. San Francisco: The Sierra Club, 1971.

'Yurok Tribe Built Its Houses of Redwood in Early Days.' *Architect & Engineer*, March 1940, pp. 43–44.

INDEX

Page numbers in italics refer to illustrations

Photograph and illustration credits

CHUCK PLACE: back cover & back flap (jacket); 5, 10, 20, 24, 32 (center), 34 (top), 35, 41 (center), 46, 47, 50, 54 (right), 55, 58, 59, 62, 63 (bottom three), 65, 68, 69, 80, 135 (bottom), 150, 152 (Colour), 155, 157 (bottom), 160, 162, 163, 168 (top), 178, 179, 182.
DEWITT JONES: front cover (jacket); 2, 3, 32 (bottom right), 42 (no 2), 54 (left), 63 (top right), 130, 131, 134, 135 (top), 138 (top right), 167 (right), 170 (center right), 173 (bottom), 183.
LARRY ULRICH: 6, 14, 21, 28, 29, 34 (bottom), 41 (top), 42 (no 3), 46 (top left), 47 (top center right), 169. 172, 175 (bottom).
US NATIONAL PARK SERVICE: front flap (jacket); 4, 44 (margin), 45 (margin), 49 (bottom), 88, 138 (center left), 159. THOMAS WEIR: 8. JIM WARGER: 9, 11, 17, 25, 51, 73, 81, 151. SUSAN NERI: 12, 13.
JON GOODCHILD: 15, 16, 18, 20, 22, 27, 31, 32 (top & bottom left), 37, 41 (bottom left), 43 (no 4), 53, 72, 77 (bottom left), 137, 138 (center right), 139, 143, 145, 147 (left), 149 (top), 161, 170 (top), 171, 173 (top).
REDWOOD EMPIRE ASSOCIATION: 18, 33, 36, 43 (no 5), 45, 97, 185. US LIBRARY OF CONGRESS: 19.
SOURISSEAU ACADEMY OF SAN JOSE STATE UNIVERSITY: 26, 33 (bottom), 85 (top), 94, 106, 149 (bottom), 153 (top), 158.
SAVE-THE-REDWOODS-LEAGUE: 37 (bottom), 48, 49, 75, 76, 79, 165. DOUGLAS DAVIS: 38 (margin).
DALE HOLDERMAN: 38. CLERIN ZUMWALT: 39. FRANCIS GOLDEN: 39 (bottom).
BANCROFT LIBRARY, UNIVERSITY OF CALIFORNIA, BERKELEY: 40, 60, 61, 67 (top), 70, 71, 83, 84 (bottom), 86 (bottom), 89, 91 (bottom), 92, 95, 96, 98, 100, 101, 102 (top), 108, 109, 113, 114, 115, 116, 120 (bottom), 125, 126, 128, 175 (top).
PILOT ROCK, INC: 42 (nos 1 & 4), 43 (top & bottom right), 167 (left). ART ROGERS: 42 (bottom), 177, 180, 181. R E BUSCH, JR: 43 (bottom left), 148 (right), 164, 166, 170 (left). CALIFORNIA DEPARTMENT OF PARKS AND RECREATION: 44, 56, 67 (bottom), 84 (top), 85 (bottom), 99, 112 (top), 118 (bottom), 184. PAUL KAYFETZ: 47 (bottom right).
US FOREST SERVICE: 57. THOMAS HARVEY: 63 (top left). CALIFORNIA REDWOOD ASSOCIATION: 74, 110, 111, 112 (bottom), 132, 144. CARNEGIE INSTITUTE, WASHINGTON: 77 (top left). CHARLES R HARRISON: 77 (center), 148 (left). JEREMY JOAN HEWES: 77 (bottom right).
YOSEMITE NATIONAL PARK HISTORICAL COLLECTION: 87, 153 (bottom). WELLS FARGO BANK HISTORICAL COLLECTION: 90, 91 (top), 93, 117 (bottom). SEQUOIA NATURAL HISTORY ASSOCIATION: 102 (bottom). SMITHSONIAN INSTITUTE: 103. UNIVERSITY OF CALIFORNIA AGRICULTURAL EXTENSION: 118 (top), 120 (top).
SOUTHERN PACIFIC RAILROAD HISTORICAL COLLECTION: 119, 122, 123, 129. THE US NATIONAL ARCHIVES: 121, 154. MARK LIVINGSTON: 124. NEIL JACOBS: 132. THE SIERRA CLUB: 133, 152 (top & margin), 175 (margin), 176. PACIFIC COAST ARCHITECT: 136. CRAIG DUMONTE: 138 (top left), 147 (right). HERBERT WISE: 138 (bottom). THE BOHEMIAN CLUB: 140. CALIFORNIA EDUCATION DEPARTMENT DOCUMENTS COLLECTION: 141. THE UK NATIONAL TRUST: 142. SEMPERVIRENS FUND: 156, 157 (top). J W SHIPLEY: 168 (bottom).

Acknowledgments:

The knowledge and assistance of many talented people have gone into the preparation of this book. Special thanks are extended to Bill Henkin, project director; Jon Goodchild, designer and research wizard; Sandy Shepard, research assistant; and the resourceful and willing staff members of the Sierra Club Library, the valuable assistance of geologist R E Busch Jr of Humboldt State University, the Forestry School Library at the University of California, Berkeley, Save-the-Redwoods League, and the cartography of Rand McNally & Company.